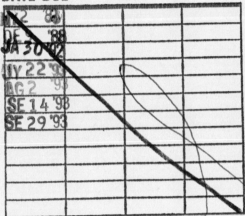

THE POLITICS OF JUSTICE

Kennikat Press

National University Publications

Multi-disciplinary Studies in the Law

General Editor

Rudolph J. Gerber
Arizona State University

WILLIAM C. LOUTHAN

THE POLITICS OF JUSTICE

A Study in Law, Social Science, and Public Policy

National University Publications
KENNIKAT PRESS // 1979
Port Washington, N.Y. // London

Manufactured in the United States of America

Published by
Kennikat Press Corp.
Port Washington, N. Y./London

Library of Congress Cataloging in Publication Data

Louthan, William C.
    The politics of justice.

    (Multi-disciplinary studies in the law) (National university publications)
    Includes bibliographical references and index.
    1. Justice, Administration of–United States.
2. Judicial process–United States. 3. Jurisprudence.
4. Social sciences–United States. 5. Public policy
(Law)–United States. I. Title.
KF380.L68   340'.0973   78-27711
ISBN 0-8046-9218-1

CONTENTS

LIST OF FIGURES

PREFACE

This is a book about the politics of justice in America written at a time when the crises of maladministration in our courts and unethical posture in those who participate in the judicial process have deepened. Believing that the study of law and legal process is much too important to be left exclusively to lawyers, I have approached the subject from a social scientific perspective which, ultimately, I label "juriscience." After introducing the concepts of law, legal process, and social science, I advance the thesis that jurisprudence was the first of the social sciences and, as a precursory discipline, provided the newly emerging social sciences with data, methods, and tools which assisted their subsequent development and for which they became intellectually indebted. I then attempt to show how the modern social sciences have begun to pay off their debt to jurisprudence by answering questions about law and legal process which jurisprudence has left unanswered. Finally, I analyze the legal process as a tool for solving policy problems and attempt to determine whether the social scientific study of questions left unanswered by jurisprudence has as yet produced a juriscience. The study of the interface between law and society is one of the most vital and urgent tasks of the American scholar in the second half of the twentieth century. Perhaps most significantly, this book addresses that interface theme by relating law (as a social policy instrument and normative policy analysis tool) to the policy sciences.

ACKNOWLEDGMENTS

I wish to express sincere gratitude, first, to my preceptor, a great teacher/scholar, Professor Francis R. Aumann. It was he who first suggested to me that the study of the law can sharpen the mind by narrowing it. His great works which stand to suggest that this need not happen [*The Changing American Legal System* (1940) and *The Instrumentalities of Justice* (1956)] have been an intellectual inspiration for me. He saved me many errors and could have saved me more if I had had his patient persistence in the pursuit of perfection.

No author can survive without assistance and I am particularly indebted to Mrs. Joanne Everhart who was tirelessly patient in typing and retyping my manuscript and to Mrs. Louise Easterday for the support of her secretarial services.

Finally but foremost my family: to my parents who have given me Life, Love, and Moral Guidance; to my wife, Leslie Koons Louthan, who gives me and shares with me Love, Nourishment, and Dreams; and to my children, Lauren and Mark, who give me Fits (usually but not always of Joy)—I dedicate this book.

THE POLITICS OF JUSTICE

PART ONE

JURISPRUDENCE AS THE FIRST OF THE SOCIAL SCIENCES

The purpose of part 1 is to introduce the concepts of law, legal process, and social science, and to relate law and legal process to the social scientific study of public policy.

1

JURISPRUDENCE AND SOCIAL SCIENCE

THE NATURE OF JURISPRUDENCE

The term jurisprudence is used in a variety of ways. In the United States jurisprudence is sometimes used merely as an imposing, polysyllabic synonym for law in general, as when we talk about medical jurisprudence (that is, all of the existing law on medicine). In France *la jurisprudence* is used to identify the course of judicial decisions (what we in the United States would term case law as opposed to constitutional, statutory, or administrative law), and this usage also is now deeply rooted in American practice due largely to Judge Story's three-volume study, *Equity Jurisprudence* (1918), which traced the development of case law in Anglo-American courts of equity. In England jurisprudence is usually used to describe the comparative study of the essential principles of law—enforced written rules—in developed legal systems.[1] This usage too has been imported to the United States where it currently describes the teaching practice in most American law schools. In this book we will employ none of the above, but rely rather upon the original and etymological meaning of the term jurisprudence as the science of law.[2]

Jurisprudence is a particular mode of study, not of a single set of laws or of all the laws of a single state, but of the general idea of law itself. Although this book deals almost exclusively with the American judicial process, we begin with a very broad treatment of jurisprudence which could just as easily serve as an introduction to the study of the judicial process in any other western nation or of a variety of judicial processes comparatively. We use this broad introductory approach for two reasons: (1) because the author is convinced that the student of American judicial process should have a rigorous grounding in the nature of law in general and its evolution in western civilization; and (2) because it is the argument of this book that jurisprudence is the first of the social sciences and that all modern social science subdisciplines which deal with legal process are indebted to the mother discipline which must therefore be understood. Thus, it would seem that the first order of business should be to define what we mean by law, but the matter is not that simple. We know that law possesses, at least, a dual nature: it is, on the one hand, an abstract set of rules and, on the other, a body of social machinery which functions to secure and maintain order in the community.[3] Or, as Roscoe Pound puts it, the term "law" designates both the legal order (rules) and the means by which the legal order is secured (machinery or process). When we speak of "respect for law" we mean respect for the legal order, but when we speak of "the Roman law" we mean to include as well the machinery by which the legal order is maintained and the process by which justice is administered.[4] The difficulty is that some schools of jurisprudence place an exaggerated emphasis on the first of these meanings, others on the second. In this chapter we will attempt to distinguish between the leading schools of jurisprudential thought and, arriving at an appropriate understanding of the boundaries of our subject, show how the law relates to public policy and why students and scholars in the social sciences must understand jurisprudence to be the mother discipline.

THE SCHOOLS OF JURISPRUDENTIAL THOUGHT

As the science of law, jurisprudence originates with the Greeks, recognizing of course that the word "science" in this context is used in the classical Greek sense and does not include a modern social science component. Nevertheless, we must emphasize that in the works of Plato and Aristotle there is no separation of legal and social theory. In their analyses of social problems, the legal and the political coalesce within the boundaries of the "master science."[5] Their study of man (later to become anthropology), his behavior (later to become psychology and sociology), and his institutions (later to become political science) are inextricably intertwined with their study of law and, in this sense, jurisprudence originates in Greek philosophy. However, from the vantage point of the late twentieth century, we are able to observe that the designation of a field of inquiry as either philosophy, history, science, or social science shifts and changes in a manner consistent with the broader, underlying trends in intellectual attitudes. Thus, as Pound points out, seventeenth and eighteenth-century scholars tended to think of organized knowledge as philosophy, nineteenth-century scholars as history, and twentieth-century scholars as science. It follows then that "when the philosophical method was dominant, jursiprudence was called a philosophy, when a historical method prevailed it was thought of as history, and under the reign of . . . [the] sociological method it has been considered a science."[6] And, even though the sociological or social scientific approach to the study of man and his institutions (including law) can be found, at least implicitly, in the study of philosophy as developed by the Greeks, it was not until the early nineteenth century when the German historicists and English positivists carved out a distinct sphere of intellectual concerns centered nearly exclusively in the law as a unique phenomenon that modern jurisprudence, mother discipline of the social sciences, first emerged. This is not to say that the leading schools of modern jurisprudence have no intellectual antecedents. The historical jurisprudents were Hegelians; the positivists, though stemming out of utilitarian philosophy, can be traced back further to (at least) Marsilio of Padua's fourteenth-century definition of law as coercive commands enforceable in the courts, and so on. Rather, it is to emphasize that the intellectual heritage of the contemporary student of judicial process and policymaking can be directly traced no further back than to about the year 1800. That is where we will begin.

The Historical School. Prior to the nineteenth century most legal thought took place either as a branch of theology or, at the broadest, within the relatively narrow confines of natural law philosophy. The emphasis was clearly upon individualism, rationalism, and universalism. The historical school of jurisprudence, first of the modern schools, was a vigorous reaction against this past. Founded by Friedrich Savigny (1779–1861) in 1814,[7] the historical school grew out of the surge of nationalism which swept across Western Europe at the end of the eighteenth century. Hence, rather than the individual, it emphasizes the spirit of the people or Volksgeist; rather than reason, it emphasizes the history of social experience as the unchallengeable basis for the legal order; and rather than universalism, it emphasizes the unique nature of a people's legal system.[8] Specifically, Savigny's historical school insists that in order to understand law one must first examine its source and only then its outward manifestations. While the customs of a community and the commands of its officials may constitute evidence that law exists, they do not represent its essence. Its essence lies in its gradual, organic, unconscious development which evolves like the language of a people and, like language, it is a singular synthesis of a nation's genius. Simply put, law is that instinctive sense of right possessed by every race.

The great strength of the historical school is its insistence that law does not exist in a vacuum and must be considered in direct relationship to the social milieu in which it develops and of which it is a part. The English historical school (in distinction from Savigny's German school) founded by Sir Henry Maine (1822-1888) has kept this theme alive, and such writers as Pollock, Maitland, and Holdsworth have subsequently demonstrated the close connection between English social history and the evolution of the common law. However, the historical school has several shortcomings. First, although some laws may be the product of unconscious growth, others clearly result from conscious efforts of various kinds. Years of conscious struggle, for example, have produced the abolition of slavery, the freedom of landed property, and much of modern trade-union law. Conscious imitation plays a large role in legal evolution as evidenced by the fact that much of the Roman law was intentionally borrowed from others. And conscious refinement of legal rules is practiced by judges who extend the law far beyond any original instinctive sense of right. Second, what Savigny calls the outward manifestations of law, customs and commands, are in fact not always based on a sense of right but sometimes on the demands of dominant interests, often even minority interests (the institution of slavery, for example). Third, the historical school does not allow for an instrumental view of law—law as an instrument for social change—because social legislation can succeed according to the historical view only if it is in accord with the instinctive sense of right of the race to which it is addressed. This leads the historical school to the normative prescription that conscious law reform be discouraged and to the normative rejoinder of its critics (such as Roscoe Pound) that the school is guilty of "juristic pessimism."[9] Fourth, even if we were to set aside the shortcomings presented above in order to emphasize the historical school's strength we would find that in the twentieth century when change is rapid and values are easily uprooted the historical school's approach is extremely difficult to apply.

These weaknesses necessarily invite reaction and criticism. For some legal scholars the historical school's principal error is its inevitable overbreadth. By emphasizing the social milieu in which law evolves, it creates a jurisprudence with such broad boundaries that the student dissipates his energies over too wide a front. This reaction gives rise to the positivist school. For others the historical school's insistence upon a theory of unconscious growth is its principal error and requires a rebuttal producing evidence that the life of the law is a process of conscious struggle and strife, a reaction giving rise to the sociological school. We will examine these two schools next and in that order.

The Positivist School. John Austin (1790–1859) is generally regarded as the founder of the positivist school.[10] Finding the boundaries of jurisprudence too broad and works on jurisprudence in a muddle, Austin adopts a method of exclusion. He confines jurisprudence to the study of law as it is, leaving the question of what law ought to be to others. Although a disciple of Jeremy Bentham and himself an enthusiastic utilitarian, Austin argues that the study of the ideal forms of law should be left to the "science of legislation," that although the context of law can be examined from a utilitarian point of view, utility is put in legal form by the "lawmaker" and this process is not a fit subject for jurisprudence. The broadest approach Austin is willing to take is to say that, simply put, law is the command of the sovereign. It is "a general rule of conduct laid down by a political superior to a political inferior."[11] In short, it is the rules in force. Austin is not unmindful of the role played by a variety of social forces in shaping the law but his intent is to make a sharp distinction between positive law (rules in force) and such other social rules as custom, ethics, and morality. This he accomplishes by emphasizing the notion of command which requires a threat of sanction by a determinate person or persons if the "law" is to be obeyed. For this reason, Austin does not regard international law as law at all because there is no determinate sovereign whom the nations of the world customarily obey. Hence, what is commonly called international law, Austin labels nothing more than positive international morality. Thus, for Austin, the boundaries of jurisprudence do not extend beyond the authoritative precept of developed legal systems; the content of jurisprudence is "the pure fact of law" excluding all reference to ideals;

the method is to analyze these rules in force and the objective is to reach a universal science of law. To define a law and analyze its logical relationship to other laws is to define law.[12]

Positivism has easily found its way to the United States. American writers have not found it difficult to replace the king of England in Austin's formulation with the concept of a "popular sovereign" and to replace the concept of command with the notion of the "public will," whereby the people elect legislators who make laws that it is the duty of judges to enforce in their decisions. The positivist lawyer's conceptualization of the law is best described by Wolfgang Friedmann as follows:

> The [positivist] lawyer . . . is not concerned with ideals; he takes law as given matter created by the state, whose authority he does not question. On this material he works, by means of a system of rules of legal logic, apparently complete and self-contained. In order to be able to work on this assumption, he must attempt to prove to his own satisfaction that thinking about the law can be excluded from the lawyer's province. Therefore, the legal system is made water-tight against all ideological intrusions, and all legal problems are couched in terms of legal logic.[13]

Although the positivist approach successfully narrows the boundaries (and thereby the tasks) of jurisprudence to more nearly manageable proportions, it tends to mistakenly magnify the inert nature of legal rules and make insufficient allowance for the creative element in the law. Law is an organic body of rules with an inherent power of growth, not a static set of precepts. It develops by taking emerging values from the community which allow it to adapt to changing popular standards of right and wrong, not by logic alone. Its content is continually derived and enunciated and must be viewed in relevant application. It does not come to us ready-made. The judge's decision is sometimes based on his "inarticulate major premise" or "social picture" of what values lie behind the law.[14] It is not based on merely analysis and deduction. Some of these problems are dealt with by the sociological school and its natural offspring, the realist school.

The Sociological and Realist Schools. Rudolf Von Jhering (1818–1892) in his *The Struggle for Law* (1879) emerges at once as the leading critic of the historical school and precursor of the sociological school. Jhering argues that law does not develop organically as does language but through the most violent struggles which often last for centuries. "All the law in the world has been obtained by strife. Every principle of law . . . had first to be wrung by force from those who denied it. . . ."[15] In this sense, as observed earlier, Jhering is a harsh critic of Savigny's historical school. At the same time, he lays the groundwork for the sociological school by insisting that jurisprudence concentrate not on the definition of law (either as a sense of right or as an authoritative command) but on the interests which the legal system protects and on how it protects them.

And hence it is that Justice which, in the one hand, holds the scales in which she weighs the right, carries in the other the sword with which she executes it. The sword without the scales is brute force, the scales without the sword is the impotence of law. The scales and the sword belong together, and the state of law is perfect only where the power with which Justice carries the sword is equalled by the skill with which she holds the scales.[16]

Jhering is the precursor of the twentieth-century sociological school because unlike the other nineteenth-century writers we have reviewed he is not nearly as concerned with the content and conceptualization of law as he is with its actual operation or functioning in society.

Indeed, the basic tenet of the sociological school is that one cannot understand what a thing is unless he understands what it does.[17] Thus, for Roscoe Pound (1870-1964),[18] generally considered the founder of the school, law is not merely a command or an abstract sense of right but "a process of balancing conflicting interests and securing the satisfaction of the maximum of wants with the minimum of friction."[19] The emphasis is clearly on process not content (customs, commands, codes) because, as Eugen Ehrlich has observed, "to attempt to imprison the law of a time or of a people within the sections of a code is about as reasonable as to attempt to confine a stream within a pond."[20] Not what the courts say but what they do and how they do it is the proper subject of jurisprudence. And further, argues Pound, the positivist's conception of a mechanical judicial process in which the courts operate with adding-machine accuracy is not how they do it. Courts do consider such questions as those of convenience and social interest and so must jurisprudence. It must be emphasized, however, that for the sociological school, when courts perform such functions which relate to the ends or purposes of law they do not rely on abstract ideals or divine guidance but make tentative compromises valid only for the present generation based on particular and contemporary community standards. Pound describes the program of the sociological school as follows:

Beginning with the proposition that the legal order is a phase of social control and to be understood must be taken in its setting among social phenomena, [we] urge study of the actual social effects of legal institutions and legal doctrines; sociological study in preparation for lawmaking; a sociological legal history in which the social background and social effects of legal precepts, legal doctrines and legal institutions in the past shall be investigated; and above all study of how these effects have been brought about.[21]

Pound's studies of the actual functioning and effects of law lead him to find over and over again that law in action is quite commonly different from law in the books.[22] This discovery has in turn led a group of scholars, usually called the realists, to branch off from the sociological school and to devote their energies to documenting the element of uncertainty in the law. The realists regard Pound has having come face to face with reality but as having failed to appropriately apply his discovery to the study of law. Oliver Wendell Holmes is occasionally regarded as the intellectual ancestor of the realist school because of the fundamental skepticism which weaves its way through all of his writings. "The life of the law," he writes, "has not been logic: it has been experience."[23] By this epigram he means to express his studied observation that, due to a variety of factors (most notably the personal characteristics of the judge, his intuitions and biases), there is great uncertainty and confusion in the law. Hence the law cannot be meaningfully treated through the use of the syllogism as if it were nothing more than a series of axioms in a book of mathematics. It must be treated rather as the history of judicial decisions; decisions based on "the felt necessities of the time, the prevalent moral and political theories, [and] intuitions of public policy."[24] Thus, for Holmes, when it comes to the study of the law, a page of history is worth a volume of logic. However, for Holmes, realism is not a method; it is merely a mood or spirit, specifically, the temperament of turn-of-the-century pragmatism.[25] For this reason, not Holmes but Benjamin Cardozo is properly considered to be the bridge between the sociological and realist schools. Although Cardozo's work taken as a whole, like Holmes's, fits much more neatly into Pound's sociological school than it does into the realist school, his emphasis on psychology and his use of psychological realism in the study of the judicial method (why judges in fact decide cases as they do)[26] is the most enduring theoretical contribution of the sociological/realist approach and is, without question, the forerunner of judicial behavioralism in political science. (Cardozo's theory of judicial method as a precursor of modern judicial behavioralism is dealt with in detail in chapter 3.) At the same time, by emphasizing psychological variables Cardozo further undermines the mechanical adding-machine theory of judicial method put forth by the positivists (and first criticized by the sociological school), paving the way for the new movement led by Karl Llewellyn and Jerome Frank which we call realism.

Realists insist that law be defined in terms of official action. Like Pound, they argue that we must study what courts *do,* not what courts say. But they broaden the boundaries of jurisprudence far beyond anything Pound would tolerate. Since "the law" is whatever the courts say it is, it follows that any variable related to why judges decide as they do (whether, as Paton puts it, "corruption, indigestion, or partiality for the other sex")[27] is a proper subject for jurisprudence. It is true that realism as a movement is comprised of heterogeneous scholars and has no fixed creed. Indeed, Llewellyn insists that is not even a distinct school[28] and Frank prefers to be called a "constructive legal sceptic" rather than a realist. But realists are united in: (1) their rejection of "traditional jurisprudence," its verbalism and scholasticism, and its tendency to be deceived by what courts say; (2) their method with its emphasis on the need for objectivity and reliance on statistics; and (3) their determination to document the element of uncertainty in the law. Llewellyn is what Glendon Schubert calls a "rule skeptic"[29] because his work deals largely with the uncertainty produced in the actual operation of the rules in appellate courts. Frank is what Schubert calls a "fact skeptic"[30] because he attributes the law's uncertainty to the broad discretion possessed by trial court judges and to their frequent use of faulty judicial techniques in the discovery of the facts.[31] These emphases on extralegal forces (such as the judge's postlunch indigestion), on ambiguities in the rules as actually applied by appellate judges, on errors in fact finding by trial judges, lead the realist school to conclude that law can be understood as nothing more than that which courts or other legal officials, for whatever reason, actually do.

The sociological and realist schools instill new life into the study of law. They force us to study, at least in part, the social interests which law actually protects and they provide us with a new understanding of the judicial method. But like the other schools, they have shortcomings. There is a tendency, at least among the more zealous, to study everything except the law itself. Again, as is the case with the historical school, this tendency produces a jurisprudence of such breadth that the student dissipates his energies over too broad a front. And again, reaction sets in; this time in the form of the pure science school. Also, sociological, and more particularly, realist jurisprudence gives inadequate attention to the ideal ends or purposes of law. In its search for objectivity, the realist school concentrates on what is, and largely ignores the question of what ought to be. There are those who argue that such a jurisprudence provides only an illusion of reality because reality, in the final analysis, includes the ought. The search for ideal ends is the objective of the teleological school. We will examine these last two schools next. There is an additional problem with the sociological and realist schools that is more appropriately discussed later. This is the observation that the sociological and realist schools never solve the problem of method. They appear in the evolution of the study of law when the other social sciences are just being born and are not yet prepared to assist in the sociological study of law. The story of how the new social sciences pay off on their debt to jurisprudence, the mother discipline, by answering questions about the nature of law and public policy which jurisprudence left unanswered is the subject matter of this book and is summarized in the concluding chapter.

The Pure Science School. The leader of the pure science school is Hans Kelsen (1881-).[32] Kelsen has one and only one objective in common with the realists: the search for objectivity. But whereas this leads the realists to broaden both the content and the methods of jurisprudence, it leads Kelsen to narrow the boundaries in the Austinian tradition. His desire is to produce a pure theory of law free from all "irrelevant material," which means both subjective speculations (such as speculations relating law to social values like justice) and social scientific data (such as empirical findings concerning judicial method). He wants to divorce the study of law from all considerations of ethics, social philosophy, and social interests. To achieve his objective, Kelsen goes far beyond Austin in narrowing the boundaries of analysis by refusing to adopt Austin's definition of law as the command of the sovereign. This definition raises subjective and political questions (for example, why are some laws obeyed while others are not?) and he wishes his theory to be entirely objective. Issues of authority and compliance with authoritative commands may be interesting but they are not to be studied by students of jurisprudence.[33]

So Kelsen reduces his theory to a much narrower base than that of Austin. The law is nothing more than a system of abstract norms emptied of all practical content. It is true that judges have discretion in applying these abstract norms. And it is true that citizens have some discretion in adhering to them. But to maintain his objectivity Kelsen places these matters outside the proper scope of jurisprudence. The best short statement of Kelsen's rather impotent theory is Paton's: "The sphere of jurisprudence, then, is a study of the nature of this hierarchy of norms, the validity of each norm depending on its being laid down in accordance with a superior norm until we reach the initial hypothesis which jurisprudence can only accept and cannot hope to prove."[34] Most students of jurisprudence agree that Kelsen's contribution lies in the fact that he helps to expose "politics masquerading as jurisprudence." That is, he does demonstrate that a pure, universal theory of law is possible and in the process he shows that what many writers had labeled principles of law were in fact nothing more than statements of their own political philosophies and prejudices. However, Kelsen's method removes all the doubts and difficulties which comprise reality and make any theory of law worth having. He gives us dry bones, no flesh and no blood.[35] We need the empiricism of the sociological and realist schools in order to locate for any legal community the "initial hypothesis" which Kelsen cannot find. And we need the speculation of the teleological school in order to find those scales of values by which the validity of his otherwise empty norms can be judged.

The Teleological School. Most of the work of the teleological school lies in the sphere of philosophy. Its method is philosophic and it contends that even though jurisprudence may be a social science, most of the important work which remains to be done in jurisprudence is philosophic. But since philosophy overlaps most schools of jurisprudence to some degree the term "philosophical school" is inappropriate. "Teleological" applies because the term accurately reflects the principal thrust of the school: the search for purpose and validity. To be sure, other schools are concerned with ends, even if unconsciously at times. The positivist and pure science schools want logical consistency and symmetry. The sociological school wants to satisfy the "maximum" number of social interests. Even the realists, or at least some of them, are ardent law reformers (for example, they want improvement in the fact-finding technique). But the teleological school is more straightforward in its search for the ends or purposes of law and more absolutist in its need to discover ideal ends. While Pound is interested in the ends of law (in the sense of social engineering) he is, as pointed out earlier, essentially a relativist. The problem of the ideal end of law, for Pound, is one which ultimately relies on a theory of values and is the most difficult problem jurisprudence must face. His view is that philosophy never has found an ideal end and probably never will. The best the courts can do is to effect compromises valid only for the present community in the present generation. But the teleological school rests on a doctrine of final purposes based on a belief that design and purpose are a part of, or apparent in, nature. Law is intimately related to justice and thus the task of the teleological school is to discover the absolute criteria by which the validity of legal norms can be judged. Teleologists do not ordinarily involve themselves in the debate over how broad the boundaries of jurisprudence should be. The ends which law has served are the question for legal history. Empirical examinations of the authoritative allocation of justice (as a valued end) is the question for legal science. The ends which law ought to serve are the question for legal philosophy. The teleological school is satisfied that the bulk of the important work remaining to be done in jurisprudence is in this last category.

SUMMARY AND COMMENTARY

Jurisprudence is a particular mode of study of the general idea of law. As a distinct sphere of intellectual concerns centered exclusively in the law as a unique phenomenon, it emerged during the first quarter of the nineteenth century. But because the objectives and methods of various thinkers have differed, a variety of schools of jurisprudential thought have emerged. Using objective and method as the distinguishing characteristics, we can summarize the essence of the leading schools as follows. For some scholars, the objective is to create an abstract theory of law with the more specific intent of creating a "pure" theory which will place jurisprudence on the sure foundation of objective factors which are universally true. Their method is exclusion of all "irrelevant" factors and the boundaries of jurisprudence are narrowed. Austin's positivist school and Kelsen's pure science school fall into this first category. For others, the objective is to create a theory of law which explains the law's functions in society—as a type of social machinery designed to accommodate conflicting interests and secure order in the political community. Their method is inclusion of all factors bearing on what the law does and how it does it, seeking neither the abstract nor the universal but the real and the applied in total context, and the boundaries of jurisprudence are broadened. Savigny's historical school, Pound's sociological school, and Llewellyn's and Frank's realist school fall into this second category. Finally, there are those scholars whose objective it is to discover the ideal ends or purposes of law, to determine the criteria by which the validity of the concrete rules of law can be judged and to prescribe improvements. Their method is philosophic and unlike scholars in the other schools they rarely debate the issue of the proper scope or boundaries of jurisprudence. The teleological school falls into this last category.

At this point we might easily conclude that each approach to jurisprudence has its strengths and weaknesses and that the most productive approach would entail some sort of synthesis. Thus we might give brief mention to the relatively recent development of "Scandinavian realism" by Alf Ross.[36] Ross achieves a very compelling balance between theory and observation while still using the traditional categories of legal analysis. Like Austin, he maintains that jurisprudence is in error if it attempts to study law using philosophical assumptions and terms. Like Austin and Kelsen, he views law as a distinct phenomenon and insists that it must be rigorously separated from ethics and social philosophy as a disciplinary approach. In other words, there is a logical and analytical function to the study of law sharply distinct from the methods of studying such other social norms as those of ethics, morality, and religion. The student of jurisprudence is looking at a special social phenomenom, and must look at it in sharply defined terms which are peculiar to law as a discipline. On the other hand, however, Ross parts company with Austin and Kelsen if they maintain that there is no more to the enterprise. He insists that we must use their insights into the analysis of legal norms as tools for the analysis of legal behavior. Of course, he concludes, we cannot have a meaningful study of legal behavior (how law and legal officials actually function) without a defined set of legal norms (the rules of the game) which delineate that behavior. But neither can we study legal norms in a meaningful way unless they are posited on specific attributes of human behavior. The study of rules without reference to their relevant application is illusion; the study of application without reference to the guiding rules is confusion. As a social science, jurisprudence must advance our knowledge of both.

Hence we can best proceed by marking out the boundaries of our study as follows. Jurisprudence is the sociological analysis of the concepts and rules which legal systems develop and legal actors apply and of the social interests which law protects. It is appropriate that our formulation of jurisprudence contains a positivist element (concepts and rules) because as political scientists we are concerned with official, institutional action. It is also appropriate that it emphasizes the behavior of participants in the legal process (actors) and the social interests which are affected because as social scientists we are concerned with human behavior and its impact on public policy. But the introduction of social interests brings up the question of values. So our study will not be value-free. The process (sociological) of authoritatively (positivist) allocating justice as a valued end (teleological) is our subject.

This delicate synthesis of approaches enables us to watch legal actors function as public policy-makers. But first we must come to appreciate how jurisprudence, as we have defined it, has set down a social scientific foundation for the contemporary analysis of legal development and of the judicial policy-making method. This we accomplish in chapter 2. What we will learn is that by the 1950s the modern social sciences, particularly political science and sociology, became deeply indebted to jurisprudence as their mother discipline. In the 1960s and 1970s they have begun to pay off on that debt. The results of that effort are the story of parts two and three.

2

THE ANTHROPOLOGY OF LAW

THE UNIQUENESS OF LAW

Given the keen competition which continues between the leading schools of jurisprudence, it should not be surprising that the contemporary student of American judicial process will find it difficult, even today, to state exactly what the law is. It is true of course that law is not alone in its inability to supply an easy answer to the fundamental question of its essence. What is poetry? What is art? Such questions pose similar problems of definition. But as William Seagle points out, there is a great difference between the problems of defining poetry and art on the one hand and the problem of defining law on the other. No one is incarcerated for his inability to state why a particular painting is art. But it is inappropriate, at least, that one should bear the agony of being executed if we cannot state clearly what the law is.[1] We can arrive at a satisfactory definition, however, if we remember that the function of a definition is not necessarily to exhaust all of the complexities of a particular phenomenon but merely to state its essence. The essence of law is that it relates to human conduct. We need only to distinguish law from other norms relating to human conduct such as those of ethics and public morality in order to get at a useful understanding of our subject.

Ethics emphasizes the individual, the excellence of individual character, and is concerned with the impact on the individual of his compliance or noncompliance with ethical norms. Hence the motive or state of mind of the individual while complying with ethical norms is critical. Even when a legal statute requires intent for liability, it will often infer intent from conduct. For example, the person who drives his car at 60 m.p.h. in a 25 m.p.h. zone and accidentally kills a child crossing the street may be entirely free from ethical wrong. He should not have been speeding but he did not intend to kill the child. The law, however, may find him guilty of vehicular manslaughter. Ethically, he may not have intended to kill the child but, legally, his intent is inferred from the wrongful conduct of speeding. The law is more concerned with the social consequences of an individual's conduct than with its impact on his character. Ethics is enforced from within. Its value depends on the voluntary nature of compliance. Even though the "work ethic" or the "commitment ethic" may have social consequences, their value lies in the individual's voluntary compliance. Law cares little about volunteerism. The value of compliance with legal norms lies in the social benefits produced. Hence laws are enforced by force from without.[2]

Just as law can be distinguished from philosophical norms such as ethics it can be distinguished from social norms such as public morality, but the task is more difficult. Public morality, like law, is composed of rules adopted in the life of the community and hence, like law but unlike ethics, emphasizes conduct rather than intent. We can dislike being required to use the correct utensil when eating a particular course of a meal but as long as we use it the requirement is met. And like law, public morality is enforced not from within the individual but from without, not by the state but by the unorganized yet effective sanction of public opinion. Neither is there necessarily a difference between the content of law and the content of public morality. They may not be coterminous but they do overlap. Still, there are at least two clear-cut distinctions. Public morality is imprecise. It lacks the capacity to govern difficult situations. Law is expressed in precise, often nearly technical, language. It possesses the machinery necessary to determine the outcome and to rule on difficult matters. Paton provides an example: if person A who is ill and alone is dependent on person B, a close relative, for the necessities of life, and A is so thoroughly neglected by B that death ensues, is this a legal wrong or merely a breach of public morality? The answer is that public morality is never precise enough to draw the lines of obligation in such a case, but the law (maybe correctly or maybe incorrectly according to teleological standards of justice) will always be able to clarify the precise extent of legal duty. It would be possible, of course, for a legal system to simply declare that all the prevailing rules of public morality are the law and the two sets of norms would be coterminous. But in the real world there would result an impossibility of enforcement. This suggests the second distinction between law and public morality, and one which also distinguishes law from ethics, namely, the law's need to rely on force for enforcement.[3]

So the rules of law have much in common with other types of rules. Rules of law, rules of ethics, and rules of public morality are all norms, or standards of conduct. But they are not all legal norms. Legal rules possess at least one characteristic which the others lack: the reliance upon force. The execution of force, however, cannot be ad hoc or anarchic or it would lack the order which also characterizes a system of laws. Hence, the use of force is restricted to politically organized government. So law, like ethics and morality is normative; it prescribes the scope of permissible conduct. Like morality, it is positivist; it imposes sanctions as the consequence of misconduct. But these normative and positivist characteristics do not provide its uniqueness. Rather, it is the requirement that the sanctions are imposed exclusively by politically organized government that distinguishes law from other rules of conduct. In short, law is an instrument for regulating human conduct and for securing order among the conflicting interests of society through the use of sanctions imposed by politically organized government.[4]

THE EVOLUTION OF LAW: A TYPOLOGY

The rules of law do not come to us ready-made: they evolve, as the historical school correctly observes, from the mists of the past. It has been the task of early jurisprudents, precursors of modern anthropologists, and of the modern anthropologists themselves to explain the process by which a consciousness of "law" and "lawfulness" arises in human minds. As we survey their findings we notice that it is an error to assume that there is a universal pattern of legal evolution, that every legal system passes through the same phases of development in the same way. But, we can observe that at analogous levels of socioeconomic development, the essential legal institutions are very much alike. In fact, from this point of view of ever-increasing socioeconomic complexity, three types of law can be clearly distinguished: the primitive, the archaic, and the mature. This is Seagle's typology and it is representative of the commonly accepted categories today. But there are others. Paton, using a similar approach, observes four distinct types: primitive, middle, classical, and postclassical. Sir Paul Vinogradoff, in his *Outlines of Historical Jurisprudence* (1922), uses an organizational rather than a socioeconomic scheme to distinguish five types: the law of the tribe, the city, the church, the contractual association, and the collectivist organization. Seagle's typology appears most useful for our purposes.

Primitive Law. To search for the origins of law in primitive societies we must not look through the law-laden eyes of our own culture because "primitive law" is not really law at all but merely the customary means by which social problems are handled in prelegal cultures. We are dealing here with preliterate and preagricultural societies in which the economy is that of the hunter and herdsmen and in which there are only vestigial forms of political organization and certainly no juridical institutions. We are dealing here with societies based upon kinship or tribal organization not upon the territorial or political organization which is essential for "law" as we have defined it. Obviously then, we cannot label the rules by which these people live "law." However, we can look at the great, formless body of custom which exists in primitive cultures and identify those modes of coping with social conflict which are embryonically legal.

Clearly, we are observing a process of evolution; not a process by which the substantive content of primitive custom becomes the substantive content of law at some later stage but a process by which the modes of dealing with conflict through organized force, become systematized through increasingly sophisticated forms. The key touchstone of emerging law is the secularization of custom and ceremonialism. For example, one of the great primitive wrongs is sorcery. Most scholars now agree that the primitive person is capable of distinguishing between merely religious norms and secular norms. The punishment for violating religious norms is spontaneous and supernatural. It is only when black magic (a religious wrong) is punished as sorcery (a secular wrong) by the anticipated, planned, organized force of the community that a public sanction has been added to what was previously a religious rule. It is true that some early scholars like Sir Henry Maine believe there to be a phase in which religious and secular rules are intertwined and indistinguishable to the primitive person. And others, like Bronislaw Malinowski, argue to the contrary that not only can the primitive person distinguish between religion and custom, he can also distinguish between those customs based on a system of reciprocity and those which are not, and that he regards only the former as binding. But today most scholars reject both Maine and Malinowski on this point and agree that there is an "automatic sway" of secular custom whether based on reciprocity or automatically adhered to.[5] The point to be made is that primitive secular custom is incipiently legal and through the process of retaliation for secular wrongs custom is molded into law.[6]

Just as necessity is the mother of invention, Seagle writes, *breach* is the mother of law. Or, as the cliché would have it, "the greatest law-makers are the lawbreakers." In other words, law and custom are not identical. Custom is only embryonically legal. When a custom is broken and the organized force of the community is used to punish the wrongdoer and to deter potential wrongdoers, the beginnings of law emerge. It is for this reason that primitive reciprocity is not generally regarded as an early form of law. It is, in some instances, an important custom but it is not law. Reciprocity exists in civilized societies also, but it creates a social not a legal relationship. Law "has its origin in the pathology of social relations, and flourishes only when there are frequent disturbances of the social equilibrium.... Custom is ... spontaneous and automatic, law is the product of organized force."[7] The act of organizing force is initially ceremonial. Primitive societies are already acquainted with many forms of religious ceremonialism; they must only adapt them to secular objectives. Usually, this adaptation is first made in order to moderate or mitigate the blood feud (the endless series of indiscriminate murders, clan against clan). The blood feud as a means of redressing grievances is still anarchic, clearly prelegal. But over time, clans will limit the feud to a single act of retaliation and eventually to a single act of retaliation against only the actual perpetrator rather than against any member of the perpetrator's clan. Eventually, ceremonial forms of redress develop such as the so-called expiatory encounter in which the perpetrator submits himself to a volley of spears. For lesser offenses he may be permitted to protect himself with a shield or even by throwing rocks at the "spear chuckers." In more advanced stages ceremonialism functions to protect private property (for example, placing a symbolic mark on the bark of a tree to indicate ownership) and to atone for private wrongs (for example, "composition," the primitive practice of giving a feast in reparation for wrongdoing which, of course, is the forerunner of the payment of damages). It is only in the later stages of the primitive phase that this distinction between "public law" and "private law" exists. There are now some offenses (homicide, sorcery, breach of exogamy) which are regarded as outrages against the entire community and require punishment by the entire community. Only expiatory encounter or a mandatory ceremonial suicide or perhaps an organized duel will suffice. But there are other offenses, usually minor personal affronts, which can now be redressed by composition. In the final stages, composition often becomes compulsory.[8]

Still, however, since there is no form of political organization there are no courts as we know them. The individual has legal rights and duties only to the extent that he is a member of a clan or tribe and the system is held together by the fundamental unity of the kinship group. The appearance of courts to officialize the law is the distinguishing characteristic of the archaic phase.

Archaic Law. Not the appearance of writing but the appearance of courts distinguishes the archaic from the primitive phase of the law's development. In socioeconomic terms, archaic law is the law of feudalism and slavery and of peoples whose economy is basically agricultural though beginning to be rudimentarily commercial. But this is to get ahead of the story. Though a settled agriculture may be the sine qua non of political organization and hence juridical institutions, it is not the single cause. Anthropological research now supports the so-called conquest theory.

The strength of the conquest theory is that it explains the growth of law so much more persuasively than any factor of internal development. The mixture of races resulting from conquest must have led to sharper conflict than any internal process of class differentiation. The latter could not, like the former, destroy so readily the kinship bond. But a conqueror's peace could be imposed where the peace of the kindred had until then prevailed. Stern "government" became necessary when violence disrupted normal relations. The conquered would struggle to preserve their own customs while the conquerors would seek to impose theirs.... Custom would thus become transmitted into "law."

. . . .

It was the court really that launched the "state," for it was in the court that the sentiment of etatism, with all its devotions and loyalties, was first nurtured. The court was responsible for the etatistic myth because it was only through its officials that the common man was brought into contact with authority. The only "social service" ... performed by the governing class was the administration of justice. The waging of war and the collection of taxes, the only other functions of early government, were more difficult to disguise as civil sacraments.[9]

Sir Henry Maine states this explanation in the form of a paradox: the sequence in the development of law is from judgment to custom to legislation. Obviously, the substance of the customs exists prior to the appearance of courts, but in the archaic phase, customs must be declared law by courts to obtain the etatistic stamp of approval. For this reason there is no law until there are courts.[10] Indeed, some jurisprudents have argued that the actual rules of law are "secondary and unessential.... The administration of justice is perfectly possible without law at all."[11] The substance of the rules of law change but the courts, those persons who dispense the rules, remain the same. Law is not absolutely essential to the administration of justice...."[12] Courts are!

As these courts begin to declare and enforce substantive rules, a "body of law" or "corpus juris" develops. Over time this body of law stabilizes, the rules of law are coherently and symmetrically arranged, and the outcome of cases becomes predictable and certain. In the life of a community this process produces a variety of positive values: stability, coherence, symmetry, predictability, and certainty. The people know what the law is; there is order, and this is good. At the same time, however, there is a gradual growth of rigidity and technicality. The law loses its spontaneity and its capacity to grow in harmony with the life of the community which is continually undergoing social change. As we have seen, the law cannot for long remain out of step with popular standards of right and wrong, justice and injustice, and still endure. The law must change, but to change is to sacrifice those already well-established positive values of stability, certainty, and order. Hence, the perplexing problem: how can the law change yet appear to be changeless? How can it grow in harmony with the social forces which shape the life and demands of the community yet preserve the image of certainty? In short, how can the community enjoy both stability and order on the one hand and a body of law which accords with changing conceptions of justice on the other? In the development of the law there have been three ways in which this problem has been addressed: the development of the legal fiction, the creation of equity law, and the use of legislation. Although these techniques are not confined to any one phase of development, equity and legislation are predominantly characteristics of the mature phase (and will be discussed later) while the fiction emerges during the archaic phase.

The fiction, as Sir Henry Maine defines it, is any assumption which conceals the fact that a rule of law has undergone alteration, its letter remaining unchanged, its actual operation being modified.[13] For example, in the early common law the established rules of civil procedure sometimes left a victim of wrong without a remedy. If his horse were stolen he could initiate a criminal action against the thief but he had no civil remedy, under existing rules, to recover his horse. There was, however, an established rule of procedure which allowed a person who had lost an item of personal property to sue anyone who had found the item but refused to return it. It did seem absurd to many, of course, that a person could recover lost but not stolen property. Obviously, the rule of procedure could have been changed to create a new form of civil action but this would result in a loss of stability and order. Hence, a procedural fiction was created. The victim of theft could recover stolen property from the thief by alleging that the wrongdoer had found his property and refused to return it. The court would pretend that the property had been found rather than stolen. The rules of law remain unchanged; their actual operation has been modified and a more "just" result achieved. Fictions, however, are not without defects. They are useful as agents of development when stability is desired but change is also imperative. But sometimes sight is lost as to why a fiction was initially created and it may eventually be used for purposes not originally contemplated. Also, over time, fictions make the body of law, though stable, very cumbersome and almost impossible to classify.[14] Nevertheless, as a means by which lawyers can attempt to keep the law a trade secret, fictions experience teeming growth in the mature phase.

Mature Law. Just as the appearance of courts to officialize the law distinguishes the archaic from the primitive phase of the law's development, the appearance of lawyers to professionalize the law distinguishes the mature from the archaic phase. Mature law is the law of the modern industrial state and is closely connected with the enormous expansion of embellished systems of written pleadings (complex written statements setting forth to the court the claims of the plaintiff and the answers and possible counterclaims of the defendant). Though writing appears during the archaic phase, the elaborate extension of written laws and legal documents occurs only after the appearance of lawyers. Lawyers love the written word. Early in this phase when laymen were generally illiterate, complex written forms gave the lawyer an advantage and even in the modern state, they help him "preserve unto himself" the capacity to practice law. And besides, how better to maintain for the law its semblance of certainty than to write it down in books?[15]

Prior to the mature phase the principal form of substantive rules of law was precedent, the decisions of courts—case law. In the mature phase, though precedent is plentiful and is reported in big and little books all bound to appear intimidating, the bulk of the law is found in statutes (legislation), consolidations, codes, textbooks, and restatements. A statute is a legislative act which creates new law. A consolidation is a combination in a single volume or set of volumes of all of the statutes relating to a given subject. A codification is a similar combination in a series of volumes which systematizes case law as well as statutes. Statutes, codes, and consolidations are all authoritative—they have behind them the sanctions imposed by government. Textbooks (or "juristic writings" as lawyers call them) attempt to order, criticize, and generalize about the principles which underlie formal rules of law. Restatements, generally a cooperative effort of judges, lawyers, and legal scholars, attempt to restate in short, block-letter sections the great mass of judicial decisions. No authorities are cited (thus restatements differ from textbooks) and the short summaries of law are sometimes followed by illustrations, comments, or even by proposed model codes. In the United States, the best example is the American Law Institute's *Restatement of the Law*. Textbooks and restatements have no authority except that which they gain from prestige. But there is considerable evidence that courts and legislatures are greatly influenced by them.[16] Of course, all this legislating, consolidating, codifying, and restating is done in the name of simplifying and democratizing the law and making it more easily accessible to the layman, and more nearly in accord with society's changing values. But the record of mature systems suggests a paradox: though the summary of all law in a few volumes on a few shelves in the public library may make the law easier for the layman to find physically, it tends not to simplify the legal game but to give the judge all that much additional material with which to work, and being free now of the technical limitations imposed by the strict demands of applying precedent he can make the law all that much more intellectually incomprehensible to the layman. The perpetual refinement of the law in mature systems has made the law less rather than more democratic.[17]

One of the more peculiar and perplexing developments which takes place in the mature phase is the creation of "equity law" (referred to earlier as one of the means by which the law can change yet appear changeless). Generally defined, equity law means the resort to general principles of fairness and justice whenever existing law seems inadequate. In the early stages of mature law "equity rules" and "legal rules" are sharply distinct and the legal structure is composed of both "courts of equity" and "courts of law." In other words, there are two distinct sets of rules, both theoretically valid and authoritative, though the same judge may sit in both courts.

The Honorable Justice Brown when he sits in one court can give a kind of relief he cannot give in another, and, there being rights which are "good at law" but "bad in equity," he can in his capacity as equity judge restrain himself from doing what in his capacity as law judge he would unblushingly undertake. For instance, if Mr. Smith secured a contract under certain fraudulent circumstances from Mr. Jones, Justice Brown sitting as a law judge would unhesitatingly enforce it if Mr. Smith sued Mr. Jones (for breaching a contract Jones thought he had been tricked into), but if Mr. Jones [then] applied to Justice Brown . . . sitting as an equity judge [he] would issue an injunction forbidding the evil Mr. Smith, under pain of imprisonment for "contempt of court" from seeking execution of his judgment at law.[18]

Mr. Smith has a legal right under the terms of the contract even though he entered into it fraudulently, and Mr. Jones has a corresponding legal duty to abide by the terms of the contract. The certainty and elegance of the law is maintained even at the cost of injustice. But under the rules of equity, Mr. Jones can seek relief in the form of an injunction against Mr. Smith who still has his right under law to insist that the contract be executed but who will now go to jail for insisting on its execution.

Over time, however, the rules of equity become a body of stable equity law and take on the same intense technicality and rigidity which characterize law in general in mature systems. Rather than simplifying the law, equity merely adds to its breadth and complexity. In the United States today separate courts for the dispensation of law and equity have been abandoned. Law and equity jurisdictions have been combined. Judges continue however to refer to "equity rights" and "equitable remedies" when handing down their decisions.

Our brief summary of the nature and evolution of law asserts the following thesis. Law has its origin in the pathology of human relationships. It has meaning only in terms of social conflict and the attempted resolution of conflict. In the sense that there is any discretion to disobey it, law is a kind of "minimum ethic." But the record shows that legal systems rarely attempt to actually solve social conflicts but only to reduce their intensity by setting down rules by which conflicts can be fought out.[19]

SOURCES OF LAW AND JUDICIAL METHOD

The term "material source" refers to the origins of law, i.e., that from which law derives its substantive content. The law's "formal source," on the other hand, is that from which it derives its validity. It is this latter meaning we are using here. In the modern state, law is formally created either by legislation (statutory law) or by judicial decision (case law). There is much debate in the literature concerning which of these two basic forms is superior. Those who prefer statutory law argue that: (1) it is abrogative—it can wipe out outdated or otherwise inconvenient rules; (2) it is logically arranged and can be more easily discovered (though computers now make it nearly as easy to locate precedents in the mass of case law); and (3) it is made only after lengthy deliberation as opposed to case law which may be arrived at in haste to dispose of a crowded docket. Those who prefer case law argue that: (1) it contains an organic element of growth and adaptability to changing situations; and (2) it is more practical because it derives its content from application to precise, real-world situations while statutes are merely abstractions.[20] Because the focus of this book from chapter 3 to the end is on the judicial arena not the legislative arena, we will be dealing almost exclusively with case law. And because "judicial method" is itself the formal source of case law, the study of judicial method, as both an art and a science, is our next objective. What we will observe is that the jurisprudential study of judicial method led students of the law away from "doctrinal analysis" and toward "behavioral analysis," and thus served as the forerunner of "judicial behavioralism" in the social sciences.

The actual activity of judging concrete cases and controversies is one in which the judge: (1) discovers the facts of the case; (2) declares the rule of law that is applicable; and (3) decrees the result of applying the law to the facts. According to this traditional understanding, judges find and apply the law objectively (or "scientifically") without bias or discretion.

Since they must rely on precedents and use the principle of *stare decisis* (that is, follow the rule laid down previously), judges need be equipped only with the syllogism and well-developed powers of deduction. But this traditional understanding or "mechanical jurisprudence" as some have called it, gave way to the compelling observations of the sociological and realist schools of jurisprudence during the first half of the twentieth century. The laws which judges apply, they observed, are general and abstract while the situations to which judges apply those laws are specific and concrete. Simple rules are difficult to apply to situations which are the reverse of simple. As Holmes concluded, general propositions do not decide concrete cases. And if general propositions do not decide concrete cases, who does? Judges do!

To what extent, then, is the judge's task a science? To what extent is it an art? Does a judge "sit like a kadi under a tree dispensing justice according to considerations of individual expedience"[21] and unlimited discretion? Or does he not make law at all but merely find it and objectively apply it to concrete cases? Certainly, judges do not always behave as if they are, as Hamilton said they should be, "bound down by strict rules and precedents which serve to define and point out [their] duty in every particular case that comes before [them]."[22] It is perhaps inevitable, as Bishop Hoadly said, that judges make law in the process of interpreting it. Hoadly wrote in the eighteenth century: "Nay, whoever hath an absolute authority to interpret any written or spoken laws, it is He who is truly the Law Giver to all intents and purposes, and not the Person who first Wrote and spoke them." As long as law remains one of the most familiar means of formalizing public policy, the judicial office in the United States will inevitably involve political, that is, policy-making power.[23] The value of legal realism in stripping the process of judicial decision making of all illusion, however, is sometimes lost in the often accompanying cynicism which assumes that all judges desire to bend the law to their individual whims. Such assumptions fail to "depict even dimly the subtleties of the judicial process," and carried to their ultimate conclusion would find every judge "guilty of fraud, hypocrisy, or foolishness."[24] At the very minimum, however, judges must make law in the interstices between precedents. According to the theory of the logical plenitude of the law, judges cannot refuse to decide a case on the ground that there is no precise authority in point.[25] And when there is no precise authority in point, the decisive source of the law is the judge's "inarticulate major premise" or his "social picture" of what values and policies should lie behind the law. Some realists would go further, of course, and argue that the judge's inarticulate major premise intrudes as well upon cases in which precedents are clear and well settled. Prior to the findings of modern judicial behavioralism, and taking traditional jurisprudence as far as it could go unassisted by modern research technology, the best statement of judicial method is that of Benjamin Cardozo.[26]

What does a judge do when he decides cases? Somehow, writes Cardozo, he considers precedent; he weighs considerations of social welfare; he ponders common standards of justice and morals; and he seeks logical consistency. But how is this strange compound, the judicial decision, brewed? By combining logic, history, custom, utility, and standards of right conduct. (Note that Cardozo never asks whether judges *ought* to, or ought to be allowed to, brew such a compound at all. He assumes that judge-made law is one of the existing realities of life.)

Which of these forces shall dominate in any case must depend largely upon the comparative importance or value of the social interests that will be thereby promoted or impaired. One of the most fundamental social interests is that law shall be uniform and impartial. There must be nothing in its action that savors of prejudice or favor or even arbitrary whim or fitfulness. Therefore in the main there shall be adherence to precedent. There shall be symmetrical development, consistently with history or custom when history or custom has been the motive force . . . in giving shape to existing rules, and with logic or philosophy when the motive power has been theirs. But symmetrical development may be bought at too high a price. Uniformity ceases to be good when it becomes uniformity of oppression. The social interest served by symmetry or certainty must then be balanced against the social interest served by equity and fairness or other elements of social welfare.[27]

But how does the judge know when one interest outweighs another? He acquires his knowledge, Cardozo answers, just as the legislator does, from experience and study and reflection. Granted, he legislates only within the boundaries of his competence and no doubt these boundaries are narrower for the judge than for the legislator. (The judge legislates only in the interstices, the open gaps in the law.) But "within the confines of these open spaces . . . choice moves with a freedom which stamps its action as creative."[28]

Cardozo refuses to go as far as the French jurist, Saleilles, whom he quotes as follows: "One wills at the beginning the result; one finds the principle afterwards; such is the genesis of all juridical construction."[29] Such a cynical and sweeping description, says Cardozo, exaggerates the element of free volition. It ignores "the factors of determinism which ... confine within narrow bounds the range of unfettered choice."[30] However, there is in all judges a "stream of tendency, whether you choose to call it philosophy or not, which gives coherence and direction to thought and action. . . . All their lives, forces which they do not recognize and cannot name, have been tugging at them—inherited instincts, traditional beliefs, acquired convictions; and the result is an outlook on life."[31] And there, concludes Cardozo, the matter of judicial method ends, if we are willing there to end it. Jurisprudence was, in fact, willing to end it there. Indeed, the traditional research methodology of jurisprudence would not allow it to go further. Jurisprudence had made a fine beginning. It had pointed out the direction in which the legal process subdisciplines of the modern social sciences, equipped with a new research technology, should move.

SUMMARY AND COMMENTARY

The discovery of the subconscious judicial mind (by Holmes, Cardozo, Llewellyn, and Frank) is the easiest and simplest indicator that jurisprudence was the first of the social sciences. The realist school which discovered the subconscious judicial mind served as a bridge between the traditional study of law and the behavioral study of law. Motivated by the sociological school's finding that law in action differs from law in the books, the realists sought to replace the verbalism and formalism of traditional thinking (which emphasized theory to the exclusion of method) with the skepticism and empiricism of behavioral thinking (which, in its early stage, emphasized method to the exclusion of theory). Not just the particular act of discovering the subconscious judicial mind but the broader baggage of realism as well gave rise to modern social science: (1) the search for objectivity and a "value-free" science; (2) faith in the significance of statistics and statistical analyses; (3) the emphasis on psychological variables to explain human behavior; and (4) the focus on the single or unique case. Only the last of these thrusts of realism would be rejected by modern social scientists, and even then by only some of them. Those who argue that realism was method without theory accept the realist school's emphasis on psychology but reject its focus on the unique case because of their preference for the aggregate data required for theoretical development. But others would contend that the case study remains the backbone of even modern social science research. Whatever may be the preferences of most social scientists today on this last point, we cannot help but conclude that jurisprudential realism, in both assumption and approach, was the precursor of modern social science. But the indebtedness of modern social science to jurisprudence is much greater and runs much deeper than suggested by this single debt to realism.

When jurisprudence emerged as a distinct academic discipline in the early nineteenth century it set the pattern for academic and intellectual specialization which the modern social sciences have followed in delineating their own concerns. In addition to this original impetus toward specialization, two other patterns of jurisprudential development have been mirrored in the modern social sciences: (1) the tendency of the discipline to develop in phases (or schools), each depending on a particular approach or methodology; and (2) the likelihood that the conclusions to which the scholar is led about his subject are determined largely by the approach or methodology used. In modern social science, as in jurisprudence, where the tension between theory and observation is continually acute, these developmental tendencies are particularly pronounced. But similarities in developmental tendencies constitute only the prologue to the story of social science indebtedness to jurisprudence. The substance of the debt lies in the fact that jurisprudence, as a precursory discipline, provided the newly emerging social sciences with data, tools, and methods which assisted their subsequent development.

Because law is a social phenomenon, jurisprudence produced data that would assist social scientists. Legal data are not only present among sociological data, they are basic to sociological data. Whether the scholar perceives the law as predating the state (Ehrlich's notion of *ubi societas, ibi ius*), as identical with the state (Plato's observation that without law there is no polity), or as the product of the state (Austin's definition of law as the command of the sovereign), he finds law to be present in every social context. By studying legal data, then, jurisprudents suggested to social scientists that law is: (1) a set of authoritative behavioral norms whch are related to the maintenance of social control and hence related to social engineering, and (2) a mechanism which balances competing social interests and formalizes public policy. For these reasons, then, the general data produced by jurisprudents became a part of the data

with which modern social scientists were to work. In addition, jurisprudence initiated empirical investigations yielding specific data which
corrected previously-held, philosophical misconceptions. For example,
the work of Maine, Malinowski, Seagle, and many others demonstrated
that the "state of nature" of which philosophers had written was indeed
only philosophical and not empirical, that life is much more regulated in
primitive societies than the philosophers had assumed and that the em-
bryonic forms of law can be discovered there.

Jurisprudence also produced tools and methods which would assist
social scientists. Although empirical analysis is the most important, or
at least most obvious, methodological contribution of jurisprudence to
social science it is clearly not the only one. The easy availability of legal
data, indeed availability in overabundance, not only made the legal process
an attractive target for social scientific research, it also necessitated careful
conceptualization, rigorous classification, and precise analysis. Jurisprudence had discovered that social conflict has a practical significance.
Also, to the extent that social conflicts are recurrent, jurisprudence
showed that regularized modes of dealing with conflict are required. The
conceptualization of law as a mechanism for reducing the intensity of
conflict, for example, was a theoretical step forward upon which social
scientists built. The classification of legal concepts (rights and duties,
authority and liability, etc.), although largely the product of the
positivists, became of considerable assistance to social scientists both as
models of systematization and as a mode of making nicer discriminations
of power relationships. And careful efforts by jurisprudents to distinguish
law from other norms provided social scientists with useful paradigms of
precise analysis.

But it must be confessed that jurisprudence never really solved the
problem of method. As Huntington Cairns pointed out in the 1940s,
jurisprudence as a social science is a study of human behavior in relation
to, and as influenced by, social conflict and change, but it is impossible
to study how the law operates in this context until we have a greater
knowledge of the factors which cause change in society and govern its
evolution. Pound may have been correct in observing that in the house
of jurisprudence there are many mansions, that there is more than enough
room for all kinds of scholars and more than enough work. But as Cairns
noticed, sociological and realist jurisprudence attempted to build its house
before the foundations had been laid.[32] Until the modern social sciences
(political science, sociology, economics, and psychology) could themselves

further develop, any attempt to create a science of law would have been working in the dark. In other words, the further development of jurisprudence had to await the emergence of a more methodologically advanced social science. Jurisprudence had infused legal scholarship with a new spirit of realistic analysis. It had developed some significant programs of research. And it had produced some useful empirical results. But as of the 1950s there did not yet exist a juriscience. Today an emerging juriscience has appeared and in part 2 we will examine its contribution to our understanding of the judicial arena and the behavior of its participants.

PART TWO

THE LEGAL PROCESS: THE ARENA, THE ACTORS, AND THE ALLOCATION OF JUSTICE

The purpose of part 2 is to describe the institutional setting of the American legal process and to explain the behavior of participants in that process as they make public policy and allocate justice in criminal and civil proceedings.

3

THE ARENA

THE DUAL COURT SYSTEM

Because we are governed by a "federal system" in the United States, the fifty state governments, as well as the national government, make, interpret, and enforce the law. Consequently, the American judiciary is composed of a dual system of courts, the fifty state judiciaries on the one hand and the national judiciary on the other which exist side by side reaching into every geographic section of the country with both trial and appellate courts. The powers of government in a federal system are divided between a central government and smaller, constituent governmental units. That is, there is a single independent authority for the whole area with respect to some matters (the national government) and there are independent regional authorities for other matters (the fifty state governments), each set of authorities being co-ordinate with and not subordinate to the others within its own prescribed sphere. The American dual court structure is not present in all federal systems, but for historical reasons the United States does have these fifty-one separate structures. Glendon Schubert describes the American legal system a bit differently. He writes about "municipal judiciaries" which in some cases are larger than the entire court system in small states, and about "metropolitan judiciaries" which blend national, state, and local systems. Schubert's approach raises the count of legal systems to over one hundred. But there are only fifty-one formal legal structures as we have defined them.

From the beginning, the existence of the dual court system has produced both a complex relationship between national and state courts and a significant impact on the administration of justice. The United States Constitution, written in 1787, created only one national court, the United States Supreme Court. The national judicial power was vested in this Supreme Court and in "such inferior courts as the Congress may from time to time ordain and establish."[1] The first Congress then passed the Judiciary Act of 1789 creating the initial national judiciary (thirteen district or "trial" courts and three circuit or "intermediate appellate" courts inferior to the Supreme Court) to function alongside the already existing state courts. This creation of a national judiciary constituted a victory in the first Congress for those who were fighting for a strong central government because it meant that the new national government would not have to depend on the cooperation of state courts to enforce its laws. At the same time, however, the state governments did retain their own courts thus attesting to their continued autonomy and creating the complex and struggling relationship between national and state courts suggested above.[2]

From the outset the national courts have appeared to have the better of this struggle. According to the supremacy clause of the U.S. Constitution, the "Constitution, and the Laws of the United States which shall be made in pursuance thereof, and all Treaties . . . shall be the supreme law of the land, and the judges in every state shall be bound thereby, anything in the constitution or laws of any state to the contrary notwithstanding."[3] To help guarantee this supremacy of national law over state law, Congress wrote section 25 into the Judiciary Act of 1789 which gave the U.S. Supreme Court power to review and, if need be, overturn any state court decision which had held against any claim made under the U.S. Constitution, laws, or treaties. And when the validity of section 25 was challenged in *Martin v. Hunter's Lessee*[4] in 1916, the U.S. Supreme Court held that: (1) section 25 is valid, the U.S. Supreme Court can review any state court decision which denies a claim based on the Constitution, or on a national law, or on a national treaty; (2) although state courts too can initially rule on such matters they are not "co-equal" with the U.S. Supreme Court in authority—the U.S. Supreme Court is the final arbiter of Constitutional issues; and (3) state courts are bound by Supreme Court decisions on these issues. Thus, by Constitutional provision, by Congressional Act, and by Supreme Court decision, the supremacy of the national judiciary appeared secure as early as 1816.

However, the vitality of state courts has continued over time for several reasons. First the vast majority of cases, both criminal and civil, arise under state statutes, common law, or local ordinances and hence are normally tried in state courts. Since the bulk of these cases do not involve federal questions, state judges decide them on the basis of their own state's law. The average citizen, to the extent that he or she comes in touch with the judiciary at all, is likely to have contact only with state courts. Second, state court judges have generally attempted to preserve unabashedly their independence from the national judiciary. Studies indicate, for example, that when a state court judge can find no precise authority in point in his own state's law, he is much more likely to cite precedents from the courts of other states than he is to cite precedents from national courts. State judges are particularly reluctant to cite U.S. Supreme Court rulings.[5] Third, the very existence of a dual court system has created a strategic environment in which state courts are encouraged to struggle for continued autonomy. Duality creates alternative forums from which plaintiffs can choose. Indeed, in some situations, even defendants can win a transfer from a state to a federal court. There is considerable evidence that different forums produce different outcomes, particularly when state courts strive to evade U.S. Supreme Court rulings.[6]

For the most part, however, the jurisdictional lines between these two systems of courts are respected. When they do come together, they do so only because the parties to a case have raised a substantial federal question in a state court and have exhausted all possible remedies at the state level. With the single exception of this appellate connection, the state and national judiciaries remain distinct systems.[7]

ORGANIZATION AND JURISDICTION OF STATE COURTS

The fifty state court systems differ widely in structure, in court nomenclature, and in jurisdictional rules, but a few generalizations can be made. Every state has several sets or tiers of trial courts (courts of first instance to which new cases are initially brought for hearing) and at least one appellate court (a higher court in which trial court decisions can be reviewed). At the trial court level there is usually a division between major courts and minor courts in which the jurisdictional distinction is based on the amount of money in controversy (in civil matters) or the maximum length of prison terms that can be imposed (in criminal matters). In every state, state law prescribes the organization and jurisdiction of the state's courts; either the state constitution establishes and describes the state judiciary or it authorizes the state legislature to do so. As a result, no two states have identical judicial structures and no single example can be taken as typical. But it is possible to create a composite system which possesses a degree of typicality and that effort is made in figure 1.

FIGURE 1. COMPOSITE OF STATE COURT ORGANIZATION

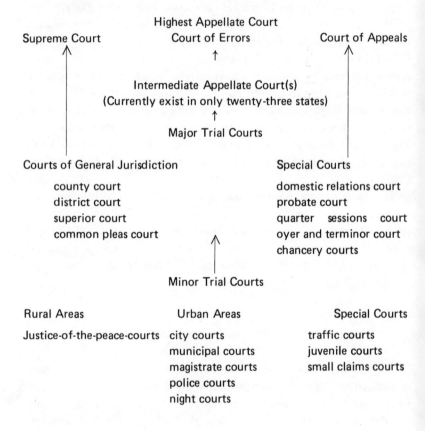

Highest Appellate Court

Supreme Court   Court of Errors   Court of Appeals

Intermediate Appellate Court(s)
(Currently exist in only twenty-three states)

Major Trial Courts

Courts of General Jurisdiction   Special Courts

     county court   domestic relations court
     district court   probate court
     superior court   quarter sessions court
     common pleas court   oyer and terminor court
     chancery courts

Minor Trial Courts

Rural Areas   Urban Areas   Special Courts

Justice-of-the-peace-courts   city courts   traffic courts
     municipal courts   juvenile courts
     magistrate courts   small claims courts
     police courts
     night courts

Minor Trial Courts. At the bottom of the judicial hierarchy in most states is the justice-of-the-peace court, particularly in rural and suburban areas. The presiding officer, the "JP," is usually an elected official and ordinarily is not required to be a lawyer. He is typically authorized to hear only minor civil cases (ordinarily cases involving a sum in controversy not in excess of $500) and criminal misdemeanors such as traffic fines and local ordinance violations. When he does sit in urban areas, he may also hear cases involving feuding neighbors, family squabbles, landlord-tenant relations, alcoholics, and building-code violations. The JP court originated in England and has existed in the United States virtually unchanged, until very recently, since colonial times. In early America, the JP was usually a person of considerable prestige in his neighborhood who had a father image which enabled him to dispense common sense justice in a predominantly agrarian society with a rather simple legal system. Today, however, the JP is likely to be a minor local politician of modest social standing, and the JP court has been greatly criticized and somewhat reformed. Since much, if not all, of the JP's income depends upon the fees he assesses against losing parties, he profits from each case that comes before him. This leads to at least two abuses of power. First, he commonly engages in advertising and in agreements with local police officers in order to increase the volume of his business.[8] Second, he generally has a much higher conviction rate in both civil and criminal cases (some studies show a conviction rate averaging 90 percent) than other judges.[9] Also, since he is usually elected by a small constituency, typically the township, he is given the opportunity to profit without fear of electoral recrimination when nonresidents come before his court.[10] Genuine concern about the problems present in these JP courts has led to the effectuation of some reform. In some states the jurisdiction of these minor courts has been limited. In others (Ohio and Michigan, for example) the office has been abolished altogether, while in still others (Oregon) the office has been abolished in some counties.

JPs rarely operate in urban areas. Cities tend to have their own minor trial courts which exist under a variety of names: city court, municipal court, magistrate court, police court, and night court. Although these urban courts, unlike JP courts, tend to have fulltime, salaried judges who are trained lawyers, they deal with minor civil and criminal matters, again limited by the amount of money in controversy or the maximum possible prison sentence. Some studies show, in fact, that the capacity of these minor court judges to serve as marriage counselors and lay psychiatrists is often more important than their legal expertise.[11] In the more densely populated and wealthy states, where both the heavy case load and the availability of funds warrant specialized tribunals, a variety of minor, special trial courts exist: traffic courts, juvenile courts, and small claims courts. In small-claims courts, no lawyer is usually necessary and, in some, lawyers are not even permitted. Although court costs are usually minimal in these small-claims courts, studies show that few people take advantage of them even when they feel cheated or wronged in a business transaction. Merchants, finance companies, and debt collectors are the most common types of plaintiffs.[12]

The various types of minor trial courts we have mentioned commonly share three characteristics: (1) they tend to be located throughout a county not restricted to the county seat; (2) they generally are not jury trial courts; the case is decided by the judge unless, in some specific situations, state law guarantees a jury trial, in which instance the case will be transferred to a major trial court; and (3) they are not usually courts of record, that is, permanent records of the proceedings are not kept.

Major Trial Courts. The second tier of trial courts in most states is made up of courts of general jurisdiction which are usually located only in the county seat. Again, they go by a variety of names but the most typical are county court, district court, superior court, and common pleas court. In these courts, major civil actions are tried for the first time as are criminal cases argued by the county prosecutor or district attorney. Occasionally, "appeals" will be heard from a minor trial court but these are not appeals in the formal sense (where a higher court reviews questions of law but not fact) because the case is tried de novo, that is, started all over again from the beginning. While a number of judges may serve a particular county or district court, a single judge presides over a given trial. All jury trials take place in these major trial courts although many cases are heard by a judge alone when the jury trial right has been waived. These are the first courts of record. Sometimes, a formal distinction is maintained between criminal courts and civil courts on this second tier. Although the procedural rules governing criminal and civil cases are clearly distinct, and although the clientele of the two courtrooms is usually quite different, both kinds of cases are regularly handled by county or district courts and judges typically shift from one court to another on a regular rotation.[13]

A great variety of associated, major trial courts exist on this second tier. In the larger states where specialization is common, we find domestic relations courts, probate courts, quarter sessions courts (courts which meet four times per year to hear criminal cases below the felony level), oyer and terminor courts (criminal courts with jurisdiction over capital offenses and other felonies), and chancery courts (courts which specialize in equity matters where the ancient law/equity dichotomy is formally retained).[14] Each of these special courts has original jurisdiction (i.e., each is a trial court or "court of first instance") in its particular area. Collectively, the various major trial courts, general and special, whatever their name, have a jurisdiction which includes (and therefore overlaps) and surpasses that of the minor trial courts.

Appellate Courts. Although every state has at least one appellate court in which trial court decisions can be reviewed, only twenty-three states have intermediate appellate courts—courts which sit above the trial courts but beneath the state's supreme court. These intermediate appellate courts are arranged in a variety of ways: in some states there are a number of courts arranged in appellate judicial districts; in others there are only two, a criminal appellate court and a civil appellate court; while in still others there is a single intermediate appellate court. In the twenty-three states in which these courts exist, appeals from trial court decisions must be directed to them before being taken to the state's supreme court. In most instances the losing party at trial has a statutory right to one appeal; as long as the appeal is properly filed, the appellate court is o-bliged to hear it regardless of its legal merit or the possible triviality of the conflict it presents. Intermediate appellate courts do not hear cases de novo, but merely receive the written briefs and listen to the oral arguments of counsel concerning points of law that were made a matter of dispute at the trial.

Since these courts consider questions of law and not questions of fact, no jury is present. The court consists of a multiple bench, customarily three judges, which makes its decision by majority vote. One of the majority judges then writes a formal legal opinion which briefly summarizes the facts of the case, the issues which the court considered, and the reasons for the court's decision. In most instances, the intermediate appellate court's decision is final. The state's constitution and/or statutes will provide for the precise circumstances under which an appeal may be made to the state's supreme court, usually only when a constitutional question has been raised. Such arrangements help control the docket of the state's highest court and free it to hear only those cases of wide public interest and of policy importance.

The highest appellate court in most states is called the supreme court, though it may be referred to as the court of errors or the court of appeals.

The greatest confusion over nomenclature is likely in New York where the highest court is called the court of appeals, and the major trial courts below, the supreme courts. Whatever its name the state's highest court is likely to be similar, but by no means identical, in both structure and procedure to the U.S. Supreme Court. It is likely to be a multiple bench typically consisting of seven to nine judges. In five states the highest court hears cases in three-judge panels as do the U.S. courts of appeals, but in the others the entire bench participates in the disposition of cases as does the U.S. Supreme Court. Like the U.S. Supreme Court, state supreme courts are the courts of last resort in their respective legal systems. Only when a case in state jurisdiction involves a federal question or when state court procedure violates the U.S. Constitution is appeal available to the U.S. Court and only then at the U.S. Supreme Court's discretion.[15] Appeal from a state supreme court to the U.S. Supreme Court is rare, and willingness of the U.S. Supreme Court to hear such appeals is even rarer. In an average year, the U.S. Supreme Court agrees to hear no more than 7 percent of the cases appealed to it from all of the state supreme courts. State supreme court procedure and practice do differ, however, from U.S. Supreme Court patterns. Some differences are glaring ones. For example, in a few states (e.g., Missouri) supreme court judges are assisted by "commissioners," appointed by the judges as their alternates, to whom they hand over some cases for decision. Formally, the decisions of commissioners are final only after supreme court review and adoption, but in practice their decisions are rarely overturned.[16] No such commissioners exist on the national level. Another difference is that in a few states, supreme courts hand down advisory opinions (answers to legal questions raised by the governor or the legislature outside the context of a concrete case or controversy) which the U.S. Supreme Court has always refused to do. Finally, the most typical distinction is that while approximately two-thirds of all U.S. Supreme Court decisions are accompanied by at least one dissenting opinion, dissents occur in only about five percent of the cases decided by state supreme courts. This phenomenon is explained at least in part by what appears to be a much greater, routine expectation, or norm, in state supreme courts that minority judges accept the majority viewpoint without dissenting.[17]

ORGANIZATION AND JURISDICTION OF NATIONAL COURTS

United States District Courts. Standing at the base of the national court system and serving as the workhorses of the national judiciary are the United States district courts. Originally thirteen in number there are now a total of ninety-seven U.S. district courts staffed by a total of 408 district court judges. There is at least one district court in every state (some have as many as four), one in the District of Columbia, and one each in Puerto Rico, Guam, Canal Zone, and the Virgin Islands. Although the existence of multiple districts within a state is presumably based on larger amounts of litigation, the fact is that some states with relatively little judicial business have more district courts than states with large dockets. For example, Oklahoma has three districts while Ohio has only two. Generally, southern states have proportionately far more districts than states in the north and the west. One explanation which has been offered for this is that since every district has appointive officers such as U.S. attorneys, judicial districting is an important source of patronage for Congress which, under the Constitution, has the authority to create district courts.[18] Although the volume of business may not be related to the number of districts in a state, it is related to the number of judges in a district. The southern district of the state of New York (which has four districts) has twenty-seven judges.[19] Idaho, on the other hand, has but one district court with one judge.

It is at the district court level that a regular, first instance trial is held, usually with a single judge presiding, with or without a jury. Occasionally a three-judge panel will hear a case on the district level. This happens when one of the parties petitions and convinces the court that an important question of constitutional law is involved in the case and that a proper disposition will probably require some sort of constitutional construction. At least one of the three judges must be a U.S. court of appeals judge from the circuit in which that particular district court is located and any appeal that might follow the decision must be directed to the U.S. Supreme Court rather than to the court of appeals for that circuit as would be the practice in single-judge cases. District courts sometimes hear appeals from the decisions of U.S. magistrates (called U.S.

commissioners prior to 1968). Although the statutory authority of U.S. magistrates (as provided for in the Federal Magistrates Act of October, 1968) differs from that which the commissioners had had and is now more nearly uniform from district to district, it is still largely limited to petty criminal offenses and such minor civil proceedings as the administration of oaths, bail hearings, and the taking of affidavits and depositions. Magistrates do have to be lawyers and members of the bar of the highest court of their state and they do have some broader authority than did commissioners—authority to hear immigration cases, most theft cases, and serious traffic cases. To date, there has been very little research on the decision-making behavior of magistrates or on their policy-making potential.

The jurisdiction of the district courts is in part exclusive and in part overlapping with state trial courts. There are basically three types of cases that are heard by the district courts. First, all prosecutions of violations of national criminal statutes are initiated on the district level by the U.S. attorney for the district. When an individual is charged with violating a national criminal law, he is arraigned before the U.S. magistrate of the district court and his case is turned over to the U.S. attorney who prepares the prosecution's case, negotiates with counsel for the defendant, and conducts the trial. The U.S. attorney does not enjoy the independence which most country prosecutors (his counterparts on the state level) have because he works at the direction of the Justice Department. Particularly in important criminal cases, he will receive not only instructions from Washington but, occasionally, Justice Department specialists will be dispatched to his district to help him prosecute the case. In an average year, approximately 50,000 criminal cases are initiated in the ninety-seven district courts. Second, civil cases can be brought to the district courts if a "federal question" is involved. A federal question exists only when it can be made to appear on the face of the record that an appropriate disposition of the case will require an interpretation of the U.S. Constitution, of a U.S. law, or of a U.S. treaty. A federal question is not raised merely by asserting a right under a national law, treaty, or the U.S. Constitution. Third, civil cases can be brought to the district courts if the sum of money in controversy exceeds $10,000 and the two parties are citizens of different states (a characteristic lawyers label "diversity of citizenship"). Diversity cases could also be heard, of course, by state trial courts and this possibility sets up a strategic choice to be made by counsel when he is "forum shopping"—choosing the court which will most likely respond favorably to his objectives. In an average year, approximately 100,000 civil cases, either federal question cases or diversity cases, are initiated in the ninety-seven district courts. It is interesting to note here that the national government is involved in civil as well as criminal actions before the U.S. district courts. U.S. attorneys handle these civil cases for the government either as plaintiff or defendant in such cases as those involving contracts for materials and services and tax disputes. In an average year, in fact, about 30 percent of the 100,000 civil cases initiated in district courts involve the national government as one of the parties. In addition to the average annual workload of 150,000 cases, the district courts also hear about 200,000 bankruptcy cases annually. But these cases are usually quite routine; the judges merely ratifying the decisions of special referees.

United States Courts of Appeals. Intermediate appellate courts have existed on the national level from the beginning. The Judiciary Act of 1789 created three "circuit courts" to sit between the original thirteen district courts and the Supreme Court. Each circuit court had three judges—one district court judge from the circuit and two Supreme Court justices. (There were originally only six Supreme Court justices, two assigned to each of the three circuits.) The term "circuit" stems from the medieval English practice by which royal justices were sent out "on eyre" (from the Latin, "to go"), to different parts of the realm. This practice was maintained in the original American national judiciary when Supreme Court justices literally "rode circuit" in pursuit of their intermediate appellate court assignments. Although Supreme Court justices no longer ride circuit, the term continues to be used to designate the eleven geographical areas served by the intermediate appellate courts of today and, loosely, as a synonym for those courts themselves.

The present structure of the United States courts of appeals exists largely unchanged since first created in 1891 and amended in 1911. The country is divided into ten circuits each of which has a single court of appeals. The District of Columbia constitutes a special, eleventh court. The number of judges assigned to each of these courts differs; one circuit has only three while another has fifteen. There are currently a total of ninety-seven court of appeals judges. Courts of appeals usually hear cases in panels consisting of three judges but in particularly important cases or when there is substantial disagreement among various members of the court, the judges may sit *en banc* (as a complete group on the bench).

As in the district courts, but unlike on the Supreme Court, the chief judge is the most senior member of the court who has not yet reached his seventieth birthday. He may remain on the court after his seventieth birthday but must relinquish his chief judgeship.

The principal task of the courts of appeals is to review cases originally decided by the district courts. Of the 150,000 cases heard by district courts in an average year, about five percent or 7,500 are heard on appeal by the eleven U.S. courts of appeals, and these 7,500 cases make up about 83 percent of its average, total workload. The courts of appeal also review cases decided by special legislative and administrative courts such as the U.S. Tax Court and the U.S. Court of Customs and Patent Appeals to be discussed below. They also have authority regarding review and enforcement of actions and orders of certain national administrative agencies and independent regulatory commissions such as the National Labor Relations Board, the Securities and Exchange Commission, and the Federal Communications Commission. The Court of Appeals for the District of Columbia is usually the busiest of the eleven intermediate appellate courts because it handles most of the appeals from the regulatory agencies, all of the appeals from the U.S. Tax Court, and also handles appeals from the District's local courts. All in all, the eleven U.S. courts of appeals hear about 1,500 cases annually from the special courts and administrative agencies producing a typical total workload of 9,000 cases per year. Like the intermediate appellate courts in the states, U.S. courts of appeals review only questions of law. There is no jury. The court accepts written briefs, listens to oral arguments, makes a decision by majority vote, and writes an opinion justifying its decision. In most cases, such as diversity cases where there is no federal question involved, its decision is final, i.e., the U.S. courts of appeals are the final arbiter of most disputes originating on the national level unless the U.S. Supreme Court deliberately brings the case within its purview. What makes the decisions and policy-making potential of the courts of appeals so significant is that only a very few cases which they decide are ever heard by the Supreme Court. In an average year litigants in about 1,500 of the 9,000 cases decided by courts of appeals attempt to have their cases heard by the Supreme Court through one or another of the channels of review to be described below. But the Supreme Court actually agrees to hear only about 150 cases, or 10 percent of those annually raised on review from the courts of appeals.

The United States Supreme Court. The United States Supreme Court is the only national court actually created by the Constitution. Although Congress is thus presumably obligated to maintain a Supreme Court, it need not provide the Court with funds and it controls entirely the Court's appellate jurisdiction. Congress also controls the number of justices on the Court. Originally set at six, the number has been changed to five (1801-07), to seven (1807-37), to nine (1837-63), to ten (1863-66), to seven (1866-69), and finally to nine again in 1869 where it has remained since. Six justices constitute a quorum.

The Supreme Court is headed by the chief justice of the United States. Although he is not necessarily the predominant member, he is the presiding member. His formal authority consists of presiding over the open sessions of the Court and over the judicial conferences (closed meetings in which the justices discuss and decide cases), assigning the writing of opinions when he is part of the majority, and supervising judicial administration for the entire national court system. He receives an annual salary of $62,500 while the eight associate justices receive $2,500 less. Unlike the chief judges in the district courts and the courts of appeals, who are always the most senior judges on their respective courts, the chief justice of the United States is not necessarily a person of prior judicial experience either in the Supreme Court or elsewhere. In fact, of the fifteen chief justices in our history only four had previously been associate justices and only two of those were on the Court at the time of their appointments to the chief justiceship. The Constitution spells out no criteria for the selection of either the chief justice or the associate justices. Legally, they need not even be lawyers, although today the political realities are probably such that no nonlawyer could be confirmed by the Senate.

The Court has typically been in session from October through May though in recent years its large docket has kept it in session through June and occasionally into July. There are basically four phases in its process: reading, oral argument, conference, and opinion writing. Much of the justices' time is consumed by reading the thousands of requests for review the Court receives each term and the written briefs of counsel for those cases it agrees to hear. It hears oral arguments in open court in most cases. During its early years oral arguments often went on for days in a single case. But by its own rule, adopted in 1849 and continuing to the present, oral arguments are limited to a maximum of two hours per case. Oral arguments are generally heard from 10 A.M. to 2 P.M. Monday through Thursday with a half-hour lunch break. Typically, the Court follows a schedule of two weeks of oral arguments followed by two weeks of recess for study and opinion writing. Conferences are held, usually on Fridays, to discuss the court's business and decide cases. These are executive sessions (closed meetings) over which the chief justice presides. He has a strategic advantage here because he summarizes the facts and issues presented, is the first to indicate how he would dispose of the case, and is the last to cast a formal vote. In the final phase, opinions are assigned and written. The chief justice assigns the opinion if he is in the majority. Otherwise it is assigned by the most senior justice in the majority. Decisions are announced in open court on Mondays.

The Supreme Court has both original and appellate jurisdiction. Its original jurisdiction is precisely spelled out in Article III, Section 2, Clause 2 of the Constitution and is limited to cases involving the diplomatic representatives of foreign states and to cases in which a state of the Union is one of the parties. These are the only types of cases which the Court can hear as a trial court, that is, without prior consideration by another court. For a variety of reasons, the Court hears very few cases under its original jurisdiction. In the first place, the Court's original jurisdiction is not exclusive. In other words, the U.S. district courts which, as we have seen, are the trial courts for the national system, are also empowered to hear these two types of cases and occasionally do so. Second, foreign ministers and ambassadors generally enjoy diplomatic immunity and rarely, therefore, are tried before American courts. Finally, the kinds of cases states are likely to bring to the Supreme Court have dwindled in recent years. During America's early years under the Constitution, disputes over state boundaries and river rights were more common, thus involving the Court in a relatively greater number of original jurisdiction cases. Today the typical original jurisdiction case in which a state is a party is one involving the diversion or pollution of water resources. But in its entire history, the Supreme Court has adjudicated only 139 original jurisdiction cases and in an average year less than one percent of its total workload is made up of such cases.

Because the Supreme Court's original jurisdiction is precisely provided for in the Constitution it can be changed, contracted or enlarged, only by constitutional amendment. Congress alone cannot tamper with it. However, while the Court's appellate jurisdiction extends to all cases arising under the Constitution, national laws, and treaties, the Constitution empowers Congress to regulate the types of cases the court can hear on appeal. Theoretically, Congress has the power to cut off the Court's appellate jurisdiction, in part or totally. Perhaps the most dramatic example of the Congress using its control over the Court's appellate jurisdiction for policy purposes came in 1869. Fearing that the Court would invalidate the Reconstruction Acts, Congress prevented the Court from determining their validity by withdrawing the Court's jurisdiction established under the Habeas Corpus Act of 1867.

Methods and Channels of Review. Prior to 1925 most cases came to the Supreme Court on what was called a writ of error. The writ of error constituted an obligatory jurisdiction; the court was theoretically bound to hear the case. As a result the Court's docket was overcrowded. It was burdened by a lot of cases which were relatively insignificant leaving it without ample time or opportunity to deal with matters of constitutional importance. The writ of error was abolished by the Judiciary Act (sometimes called the "Judges' Bill") of 1925 and the general tendency of Congressional action since then has been to contract the court's obligatory jurisdiction and to give it more and more freedom to pick and choose cases of wide public interest and great policy importance.

Today, most of the cases which reach the Supreme Court come up on writs of certiorari. Certiorari is an entirely discretionary jurisdiction. Petitions for certiorari are filed by losing parties in the U.S. courts of appeals, the three-judge district court cases, and in the state supreme courts. There is no right to a hearing in such cases. And in an average year, the Court will agree to hear no more than ten percent of the 2,600 cases petitioned. The Court makes this "cert. decision," as lawyers call it, by the so-called rule of four. If four justices, after reading the certiorari petition and studying related materials agree to hear the case, it will be heard. Four is obviously not a majority of nine, but the sense is that if four U.S. Supreme Court justices conclude that a case presents significant issues that should be resolved the case should be heard. Individual justices may concur with or dissent from this "cert. decision" but all are eligible to participate on the merits whether they had originally voted to hear the case or not. In the entire history of the certiorari jurisdiction, only Justice Frankfurter seemed to hold the contrary view that there should be no dissents from the denial of certiorari and that a justice need not participate on the merits if he had voted to deny certiorari.[20] Students of the "cert. decision" have found, as an empirical fact, that since 1925 in all cases in which certiorari has been granted the Court has overturned the lower court decision in slightly more than two-thirds of the cases. Some of these students have reasoned that such a high reversal rate may indicate that a denial of certiorari means that the Court approves the lower court decision. The justices have steadfastly denied this, insisting that the decision to grant or deny certiorari is made exclusively on the basis of the importance of the case presented. Of course, in practice, a denial of certiorari does have the effect of allowing the lower court decision to stand. The 260 cases that the Court hears under its certiorari jurisdiction in an average year make up about 87 percent of its total workload.

A second channel of review, and the only other one of much importance, is the application for appeal. Formally, the appeal is a review by right, similar to and a replacement for the old writ of error, although the conditions under which such a right of appeal exists are severely limited by statute as follows:

From the state courts
  1. Where a state court has invalidated a federal statute or treaty provision.
  2. Where a state court has upheld a state law or state constitutional provision allegedly in conflict with the federal Constitution, laws, or treaties.
From U.S. courts of appeals
  1. Where a federal law or treaty is held unconstitutional.
  2. Where a state law or constitutional provision is held invalid because in conflict with a federal law, treaty, or constitutional provision.
From the U.S. district courts (appeal direct to Supreme Court)
  1. Where a federal statute with a criminal penalty is held unconstitutional.
  2. Where judgment has been rendered in a suit to enforce the antitrust laws, the Interstate Commerce Act, or Title II of the Federal Communications Act.
  3. Where three-judge courts grant or deny an injunction in suits to restrain enforcement of state statutes, federal statutes, or orders of certain federal agencies.[21]

Although a right to appeal and a corresponding obligation to hear the case supposedly exist under these circumstances, the fact is that the Court commonly refuses to hear such cases either because the jurisdictional statement made in the application is incomplete or otherwise lacking or because the issue raised is "insubstantial." In an average year, the Court receives 60–80 applications for appeal, agrees to hear only about half of these, and the 30–40 cases it hears on appeal make up about 10–13 percent of its total workload.

In addition to petitions for certiorari and applications for appeal, cases occasionally come before the Court on certain miscellaneous writs and by certification. Certification is a process by which a lower court, usually a U.S. court of appeals, asks the Supreme Court to rule on a stipulated question of law supposedly in professional doubt. Certification does not constitute a concrete case or controversy in the traditional sense. No litigants and no counsel are actually before the Court. Rather, a lower court has merely made an inquiry or asked for instructions on a delicate matter where there appears to be no precise authority in point. If we were to count the number of cases which come to the Court in an average year under certification, miscellaneous writs, and original jurisdiction combined, we would rarely find more than ten and usually less than that.

Special Administrative and Legislative Courts. The United States district courts, the U.S. courts of appeals, and the U.S. Supreme Court are generally referred to as "constitutional courts" because they are created by Article III of the Constitution to exercise the national judicial power. As we have seen, the Supreme Court is expressly created by Article III and the district and appellate courts are created by Congress under authority granted to it by Article III. There are, however, a number of other national courts usually characterized as "administrative" or "legislative" courts which Congress has created under authority granted to it in Article I.

The United States Court of Claims hears suits for damages which are filed against the U.S. government. Most of the cases it hears arise out of public contracts. Prior to its creation, a citizen could sue the U.S. government only when authorized to do so by a special act of Congress. The U.S. Court of Claims, created by Congress under its authority to pay the debts of the United States (Article I, Section, 8, Clause 1) is composed of a chief justice and four associate justices. Appeals from its decisions go to the Supreme Court. The United States Tax Court, formerly the Board of Tax Appeals, is an independent executive agency. It adjudicates controversies involving excessive or deficient payment of income taxes, estate taxes, gift taxes, and excess profits. It was created under the authority of Congress to levy taxes (Article I, Section 8, Clause 1). Appeals are taken from the tax court to the courts of appeals. The United States Court of Customs and Patent Appeals hears appeals from import duty assessments and patent cases. These appeals come to the Court of Customs and Patent Appeals from the Patent Office in the Department of Commerce and from the customs court. The customs court itself was created by Congress to hear complaints from foreign importers who contend that they have been forced to pay an unwarrantedly high tariff. The U.S. Court of Customs and Patent Appeals was created by Congress under its authority to regulate foreign commerce (Article I, Section 8, Clause 3) and to grant patents (Article I, Section 8, Clause 8). Any appeals are, again, reviewed by the courts of appeals. Finally, the United States Court of Military Appeals was created by Congress under its authority to "make rules for the government and regulation of the land and naval forces" (Article I, Section 8, Clause 14). This court is located in the Defense Department and hears appeals from the decisions of courts-martial in which a general or admiral has been convicted or in which any armed forces personnel have been sentenced to death. It may also hear cases referred to it by the Judge Advocate General's Office. Appeals are then taken, if taken at all, to the courts of appeals.

These various legislative or administrative courts differ in several significant ways from the constitutional courts. Obviously they differ in the constitutional authority under which they are created. Constitutional courts are Article III courts while legislative and administrative courts were created under Article I. They also differ in function. Legislative and administrative courts are only quasi-judicial in nature and their principal role is to assist in the administration of specific congressional statutes. Also, Article I courts can and do issue advisory opinions which the constitutional courts do not. Finally, judges on these legislative and administrative courts are not protected by the same Article III safeguards which give judges on the constitutional courts so much independence. Article III judges can be removed from office only via impeachment by the House and conviction by the Senate. And their salaries may not be reduced once they are in office.[22]

THE POLITICS OF JUDICIAL ADMINISTRATION

At neither the national nor the state level are court systems tightly administered. In part this is due to the fact that in the United States where "separation of powers" (executive-legislative-judicial) is the underlying organizational scheme, the judicial branch has developed as a separate

FIGURE 2. ORGANIZATION AND WORKLOAD
OF NATIONAL COURTS

U. S. Supreme Court

(1) Receives cases from state supreme courts, U.S. courts of appeals, special legislative and administrative courts (e.g., U.S. Court of Claims) and from three-judge, U.S. district court panels.

(2) Receives about 2600 petitions for certiorari yearly; hears about 10 percent of these, or 260 cases which constitute about 87 percent of its workload.

(3) Receives about 60–80 applications for appeal yearly; hears about 50 percent of these, or 30–40 cases which constitute about 10–13 percent of its workload.

(4) Has original jurisdiction over cases involving foreign diplomats and states of the Union; hears cases on various miscellaneous writs & certifications, combined totals rarely exceed 10 cases yearly, or 0–3 percent of its workload.

Total average yearly workload of 300 cases.

U. S. Court of Claims

U.S. Courts of Appeals
(11 courts staffed by a total of 97 judges).

An average annual workload of 7,500 cases from the district courts and 1,500 cases from the special courts and administrative agencies. Of these 9,000 cases, petitions of one sort or another for review by the U.S. Supreme Court are filed in about 1,500 cases, and the Supreme Court in its broad statutory discretion usually hears no more than 10 percent or 150 cases.

Total average yearly workload of 9,000 cases.

U. S. Tax Court
U. S. Court of Customs and Patent Appeals

FAA	SEC
FCC	NLRB
FTC	and others

U. S. District Courts
(97 courts staffed by a total of 408 judges)

An average annual workload of 100,000 civil cases and 50,000 criminal cases. Of these 150,000 cases, approximately 5 percent, or 7,500 cases are appealed to the U. S. courts of appeals.

Total average yearly workload of 150,000 cases.

Special three-judge district court cases

body independent of the executive. In many of the nations of western Europe the judiciary is kept under careful control by a ministry of justice or a ministry of interior. But in the United States, no executive department, in either the national government or in the states, exercises such administrative control.[23] However, to the extent that administrative direction does exist within the judiciary itself it is far better on the national level.

Judicial administration is accomplished on the national level through two institutions: the Federal Judicial Conference and the Administrative Office of the United States Courts. The Federal Judicial Conference, created in 1922, helps to integrate the tasks of the Supreme Court with those of lower national courts. It includes the chief justice of the United States who presides, the senior judges from the eleven courts of appeals, representatives from the judiciary committees of both houses of Congress, and representatives from the Justice Department. The judicial conference meets annually to make a comprehensive survey of the business of the national courts, to recommend the transfer of judges from one district to another or from one circuit to another, to propose changes in court rules or other reforms, and to encourage a more nearly uniform interpretation of national laws throughout the national court system. In addition, there is a "judicial council" within each of the eleven circuits made up of all judges in the circuit to perform tasks similar to those of the judicial conference.[24]

The Administrative Office of the United States Courts, created in 1939, prepares statistics on court workload for presentation to the judicial conference. It is headed by a director and an assistant director both of whom are appointed by the Supreme Court and supervised by the judicial conference. The administrative office not only examines dockets but also compiles budgets, allocates supplies, disburses court maintenance moneys and handles accounting matters. It is, in short, the principal statistical clearinghouse and a general housekeeping agency for the national courts.[25]

It is clear that some degree of administrative clearance and control is essential to the maintenance of a viable and independent judiciary. But most of the movements in judicial administration have not been without political motivation and consequence. Studies show that: (1) policy considerations and not just the goal of greater efficiency have motivated at least some intercircuit assignments by the judicial conference; (2) judges do sometimes use the administrative system to promote their professional status and even to speak out on issues which may later reach them as a concrete case for adjudication; and (3) judicial conference policies allow national courts, in effect, to give advisory opinions (though these courts allegedly refrain from doing so) because as agencies of the national judiciary they can speak with authority (though perhaps not with finality) and the result is that the substance of law is sometimes produced by an administrative rather than an adversary process.[26] Also, a variety of studies now indicate that most efforts to "reduce the workload" of the Supreme Court to improve its efficiency have been politically motivated. Not just the Roosevelt plan to "pack the court" in 1937 but also the Taft Plan of 1925 and the Fuller Plan of 1891, and most recently, the Freund Commission's proposal of a "National Court of Appeals" to absorb some of the Supreme Court's load[27] have been shown to have political motivations and consequences. Regarding the proposed National Court of Appeals, for example, we know that the certiorari decision which would probably be transferred to the new court is a political decision, i.e., unless issues have access to the Supreme Court the values of the justices cannot be made manifest in their decision making. Hence, unless the values of the judges on the new court were identical to those of the justices on the Supreme Court, an unlikely event, there would necessarily result a change in the direction of Supreme Court policy making.[28]

In the states the plethora of courts we have described do not usually constitute an integrated system. Although some states do have judicial administrators who work under the aegis of the state supreme court, they usually do little beyond the collection of statistics.[29] There are actually thirteen states that have no judicial administrative office at all, and among existing state administrative offices, twelve were created only during the past decade.[30] This means there are practically no hierarchical controls in most states. Trial courts and even most intermediate appellate courts operate with nearly complete autonomy. Each judge is king in his courtroom. He formulates the rules under which he will hear cases, hires court personnel, and determines for himself the days and hours he will hold court. The manner and expeditiousness with which he disposes of cases is unsupervised. There is usually no statewide administrative authority to transfer judges to busy courts from less busy ones.[31]

New Jersey stands alone as a clear-cut exception to the above description. There, the state's chief justice is effectively the head of the state's judicial machinery. He has authority to require lower court judges to hold court during specified days and times and to submit weekly reports on the disposition of cases. Judges may not delay decision on a case which has been argued for more than two weeks without justifying the delay in writing. Judges may also be transferred from one court to another to help alleviate delay in hearing cases. A few other states such as California, Louisiana, Maryland, Missouri, New York, and Wisconsin have recently attempted to emulate the New Jersey model but with somewhat less success.[32]

4

JUDGES AND THE JUDICIAL DECISION

THE POLITICS OF JUDICIAL SELECTION

Judges are the most prominent and prestigious actors in the judicial arena. This is particularly true in appellate courts, but even in trial courts where judges must sometimes share decision-making power with a jury of laymen, the judges alone interpret the rules which govern the courtroom and set limits on the possible outputs or decisions. The mechanisms used for recruiting judges thus become important because judicial selection provides one of the direct means of influencing judicial policies.

Different states select their judges in different ways depending on what ideas were in vogue at the time when a state's constitution was being written or its statutes were being revised.[1] There are four basic methods. The first of these is gubernatorial appointment, in which the governor appoints all or most of the state's judges. Usually the state legislature must consent to the governor's choice. This method is most common in the East, particularly among the original thirteen states where patterns of government were well established before the Jacksonian movement to "democratize" government was felt. Today, gubernatorial appointment is used as the dominant method of judicial selection in twelve states, although in a few of these the governor's authority is limited by some sort of merit system as described below. The second method is partisan election in which candidates for judicial office are nominated by partisan caucuses or primaries and run on the party ballot at the November general election. Partisan election of judges became popular as a result of the attempt, during the Jacksonian period of the early and middle nineteenth century, to bring government closer to the people. In the beginning the partisan election method was kept "democratic" by requiring frequent rotation, terms of two or four years duration. Today, however, terms tend to be longer, ranging from four years to life (Rhode Island). Currently, twenty states use the partisan election method to select all or most of their judges. During the progressive era of the late nineteenth and early twentieth centuries, the nonpartisan election of judges became the popular method particularly in Midwestern and Western states. Here, candidates are chosen in nonpartisan primaries and then run in a general election without formal party designation. Nonpartisan elections are supposed to eliminate the alleged tendency of partisan elections to place "political hacks" in the judiciary but various studies show that in at least half of the eighteen states that use the nonpartisan judicial election today, political parties play a significant, though disguised, role. Further, it should be noted that the governor plays a significant role in many of these states because he usually is empowered to fill vacancies by appointment. Since his appointee can then run with the advantages produced by incumbency when his appointed term expires, he usually wins easily, meaning that the governor, in effect, has considerable influence over the staffing of the judiciary in the nonpartisan election states. In his study of state supreme court incumbents, James Herndon has found that more than half of those judges formally elected on nonpartisan ballots were originally appointed to the court by the governor.[2] The fourth and final method of judicial selection, and one which has become particularly popular since the organizational influence of lawyer groups developed in the 1930s, is the so-called merit plan. Generally, the merit plan is one which combined gubernatorial appointment with popular election and is assisted by some sort of "blue ribbon," judicial qualifications commission. There are a number of variations on the merit plan but the most well known is the Missouri Plan which has been advocated by the American Bar Association since 1937. Here, the governor appoints a judge from among a list of three candidates who have been nominated by a nonpartisan nominating board called the Appellate Commission. The appointment is for a probationary term of one year at the end of which the judge's name is placed on the ballot, unopposed, in a referendum election in which the question is "Shall judge (name) be retained in office as judge of the (name) court?" If successful, the judge then begins a twelve-year term. The merit plan is thought to be a response to public expectations about how judges ought to behave. Citizens want judges to be "accountable to the people for their official actions" but at the same time "free from political pressure to insure that their decisions are impartial."[3] These are often incompatible expectations but the merit plan seeks to provide accountability and independence simultaneously by combining electoral and appointment features in the same selection method. Of those states which have adopted new judicial selection methods since 1937, all but one have chosen some variation on the merit plan.

Since some form of election is now used in a total of thirty-eight states and since the merit plan is apparently the current vogue, perhaps a more detailed look at the actual operation of these two methods of judicial selection is in order. The argument for the election of judges is that judges who are chosen in popular elections with the support of political parties, overt or covert, will be more responsive to major shifts in public opinion and more attuned to social wants. In fact, we find that judicial election contests generate relatively little interest and cannot be said to produce accountability. Voter turnout is low when judicial elections are held separately from general elections for other offices. Even when judgeships are contested at the same election as other state offices, there is usually a large "roll off" (voters marking ballots for other more publicized offices but leaving the judicial ballots blank). And there is a considerable propensity in voters to select incumbents because of the greater familarity of names. Generally, terms of office are longer than for most other state offices and many incumbent seats go entirely uncontested.[4] For these and other reasons, incumbents rarely retire at the end of a term. They either die in office or some physical infirmity forces resignation during a term. Thus, the governor appoints a replacement who then has the advantages of incumbency at subsequent elections; hence, there is de facto gubernatorial appointment in what is nominally an electoral selection system. The supposed accountability proclaimed as the advantage of electing judges, is lost. Indeed, Atkins and Glick have found that in those states where judges are elected on nonpartisan ballots, 66 percent of the incumbents were initially appointed to office, and in partisan election states 40 percent were originally gubernatorial appointees.[5]

To some degree, the averred advantages of the merit plan have been shown to be similarly overstated. Supposedly, the merit plan, by infusing the selection process with the concerns of a nonpartisan qualifications board, maximizes the legal profession's desire to populate the bench with judges of superior ability. However, studies now show that: (1) although the participation by both qualifications boards and the public may limit the governor's power, he is nevertheless usually able to make appointments which "reward friends or past political supporters" and, in general, he can successfully implement the plan "very largely from a personal and political viewpoint";[6] (2) the merit plan produces judges who are not noticeably or measurably different from other judges in terms of quality of law school attended, legal qualifications measured by previous judicial experience or, perhaps most importantly, in terms of judicial decision-making style;[7] and (3) the merit plan's referendum, supposedly the point of access for popular review, has been merely perfunctory, since referenda in Missouri-plan states have rejected only six judges while confirming thousands.[8]

In short, the method of judicial selection appears to make very little difference in the types of judges ultimately chosen in the states. Although this finding might seem at first surprising, it becomes easier to grasp once we recognize that regardless of the method used, the same group of political actors (governors, legislators, parties, lawyers' groups, etc.) participate in the selection process, though the mix and relative weights of influence may vary.[9]

Judicial selection on the national level is far more simply described though just as political. All national judges are appointed by the President whose nominees must be approved by majority vote in the U.S. Senate. The President has a relatively free hand in appointing Supreme Court justices but when it comes to district court and appellate court judges he must obtain the approval of the nominee's home-state U.S. Senators, particularly if one or both of those Senators are of the president's party. This process really amounts to more than just consultation and grudging approval, it ordinarily also means that the Senator will insist on having particular candidates of his choice appointed, so that national judgeships below the Supreme Court level are quite commonly a form of political patronage for U.S. Senators. A second political consideration in recent years has been the input of the twelve-member Committee of the Federal Judiciary of the American Bar Association. When a judicial vacancy occurs, the U.S. Attorney General (who usually handles the preliminaries of selection for the President) sends a list of all prospective nominees to the ABA committee for investigation. This is supposed to happen during a six- to eight-week period prior to appointment. The committee rates the prospective nominees as "EWQ" (Exceptionally Well Qualified), "WQ" (Well Qualified), "Q" (Qualified), or "NQ" (Not Qualified) and submits

its ratings to the Attorney General. Although some candidates rated "NQ" have been nominated and confirmed many others have not. Many have never even been nominated. So the ABA does have a significant voice in the process. Still, in recent years, its influence has not extended to Supreme Court nominees. A confrontation between the ABA and President Nixon took place in 1971 concerning the ABA's "leaking" of ratings. Since then the Attorney General has submitted his list of nominees for the Supreme Court directly to the President thus circumventing the ABA committee until after the nomination of a particular person has been made.[10]

There are few formal qualifications for national judgeships. District court nominees must live in their state and district, but only at the point when they take office, not before. Courts of appeals nominees must only live in their respective circuits. For Supreme Court justices there are no formal qualifications: none of residency, none of age, none of educational or professional background. It is with Supreme Court nominees that the President enjoys his greatest freedom of action. Prior to the Senate's rejection of Abe Fortas as chief justice in 1968 and President Nixon's contested appointments of Judges Haynsworth and Carswell in 1969 and 1970 respectively, only one Supreme Court nominee had been rejected in this century (Hoover's appointment of Judge John Parker in 1930). Because these judges are appointed, in effect, for life, the President has an opportunity to influence the course of public policy far beyond the years of his own administration. There have been thirty-eight Presidents in our history but only fifteen chief justices. John Marshall was chief justice for thirty-four years over the course of six different presidential administrations; Roger Taney for twenty-eight years over nine different presidencies; and most recently, Earl Warren for sixteen years over four presidencies. Thus, the role of the national courts in making public policy cannot be exaggerated, and the power of the President to influence public policy through judicial selection should not be underestimated.[11]

JUDICIAL POLITICS AND POLICIES

The politics of judicial selection is important because: different methods give influence to different groups; different groups want and expect different things from the process; and, depending upon who has influence and who wants what, differing sets of informal qualifications are generated.

The most obvious interest involved is that of the appointing authority where the executive appointment method is used. Presidents and governors do seek political objectives in making appointments. It is true that they sometimes guess incorrectly about how judges will behave. The conservative President Eisenhower appointed Earl Warren expecting him to be a moderate to conservative chief justice. When Warren demonstrated his liberal leanings Eisenhower said of his choice: "The biggest damn fool mistake I ever made." The liberal President Wilson appointed James McReynolds thinking that McReynolds's record as a young trust-busting attorney indicated a liberal ideology. McReynolds turned out to have no other liberal bones in his body. President Roosevelt's appointment of Wiley Rutledge produced some consequences that were consistent with expectations and some that were not. Rutledge did become a defender of the New Deal as expected but he did not attempt, as had been hoped, to "form a union with Frankfurter to win back Justice Stone to the liberal wing."[12] The point is, however, that Presidents do attempt, and usually successfully, to appoint justices whose policy views are similar to their own and, over the long haul, those policy predilections are manifested in judicial decisions.[13] Although governors have been shown to have similar objectives, they are a bit more restricted in their selection of judges than are Presidents in their selection of justices. Where the gubernatorial appointment method is used, most state judges have formerly served in the state legislature where they have won friends who assist their confirmation.[14] Moreover, in recent years the better share of state legislature upper houses (which usually are charged with confirming appointments) have had Republican majorities. So, regardless of the party affiliation of the governor, governors have tended to appoint more Republicans than Democrats in all but the Southern states.[15]

Lawyer groups are also deeply involved in the selection process. They prefer judges who identify with bar associations and adhere to bar association norms.[16] As lawyer groups, particularly state bar associations, struggle for influence they are frequently opposed by rank-and-file attorneys. Governor Ronald Reagan's attempt to secure the adoption of the Missouri Plan in California provides a case in point. The plan was "fundamentally unpopular with rank-and-file attorneys who felt it would substitute the invisible politics of the State Bar for the open politics of the governor's appointments."[17] The plan was also opposed by most lawyers in the state legislature many of whom hoped for a judicial appointment for themselves. Much of this opposition, which was successful, was mobilized around the assumption that the conservative state bar leadership would offer nominees who would be exclusively conservative Republican judges.[18]

Another major set of interests involved in the selection process is that represented by political parties. For a variety of reasons judgeships are important offices for both personal and party patronage. Patronage is possible because the number of available judgeships has not been reduced in state politics, as have many administrative posts, by civil service reform. Patronage is effective because judgeships are desired by upwardly mobile minorities who want social prestige and by lawyers in state politics who want professional prestige.[19] Each patronage position in turn generates not merely a relatively high salary but a potential for influencing public policy. Judicial patronage includes as a usual minimum the appointment of clerks and bailiffs, assigned counsel in criminal cases, and administrators of estates where no will exists.[20] In some states other more important positions are filled by judicial appointment. In Pittsburgh and Philadelphia judges appoint park commissioners and members of the boards of education. And in New Jersey the chief justice of the state supreme court appoints six of the twenty-three members of the board of directors of the Prudential Insurance Company.[21]

A final set of interests involved in judicial recruitment but commonly overlooked by students of judicial selection are those interests held by sitting judges themselves. But there is now considerable support in the literature of political science for the notion that a policy-oriented judge on a multi-member appellate court will use the co-option of new personnel as a tactic in securing his policy objectives.[22] This phenomenon has gained most attention at the U.S. Supreme Court level where the policy-oriented justice, since he must share decision-making power with eight other justices, must first confront the problem of securing at least four additional votes for the results he wants. After determining a strategic plan to obtain a majority in the broad context, he may well employ a number of tactics to solidify the arrangement: capitalizing on personal regard; persuading on the merits; bargaining; threatening; and (since it is much easier for him to join in opinions with a justice whose policy goals are similar to his own) voicing an opinion on the selection of new personnel.[23] Some such efforts are successful while others are not. Justice Samuel F. Miller,[24] Justice Henry B. Brown, and Chief Justice Melville W. Fuller[25] all tried it with some success, but the one who was in perhaps the best position to influence appointments and who made the most systematic efforts along these lines was Chief Justice William Howard Taft.[26] The attempts of Chief Justice Stone and Justice Frankfurter first to oppose, then to support, President Roosevelt's appointment of Wiley Rutledge are also now well documented.[27]

Finally, a connection must be made between the politics of judicial selection and judicial outputs or decisions. We have seen that the method of selection does not appear to be directly related to decision-making styles. However, the struggle among those competing interests which surrounds the judicial selection process does help to illuminate the variables which are associated with why judges vote as they do. The judge's background, his policy predilections, his party affiliation are all ingredients of the judicial decision. Ulmer has found, for example, that in the Michigan Supreme Court (in a state where judges are elected and there is a measurable ideological difference between parties), Republican and Democratic judges tend to split strictly according to party lines in nonunanimous decisions on workmen's compensation and unemployment compensation cases.[28] This type of analysis leads us to consider again the question of judicial method, but this time from a social scientific perspective. Not willing to leave the study of judicial method where Cardozo had left it, social scientists have come a long way in answering the question of why judges decide as they do, a question answered incompletely by jurisprudence.

THE THEORY OF THE JUDICIAL DECISION

Limitations of Research Conclusions. There are many hazards in attempting to synthesize our knowledge of judicial behavior. The general thrust of most of the research we will look at here is to identify and measure the relative weights of the various determinants of the judicial decision. These determinants are the "independent variables" and the decision is the "dependent variable." Although this is now the conventional formulation, it leaves a few problems which must be recognized at the outset. First, the very assumption that the decision—treated as a "yes," "no," or "abstain" answer by a judge—is the dependent variable may be misleading. Like other political decision makers, the judge may have other options open to him that go far beyond voting.

His devices include questioning counsel during argument; making formal presentations at official conferences; sending memoranda to one, several, or all of his colleagues; having private conversations with fellow members of the court. . . . Thus if we restrict ourselves to votes as measures of committment to values . . . we ignore a sizable portion of decisional choices actually open to judges. . . . The range is considerably broader than yes, abstain, no.[29]

Further, a judge may be playing games with his votes. He may vote opposite to his primary predilection, waiting for a better or more opportune time to press his views. He may also do this as a bargaining technique, or as part of an image-building tactic to make more effective his future move in another direction.[30] Obviously, the simple correlation of a judge's attitudes or values with his formal decision in such circumstances would not produce meaningful results. Second, although there is inherent in the exercise of the judicial decision a significant element of discretion which can be utilized by the judge to secure policy objectives, there are also a number of important limitations and it has been nearly impossible for social scientists to pinpoint the discretion-fixity breaking point. These limitations include: (1) the need to experiment sometimes causes personal predilections to give way to the demands of original situations; (2) legal training, common to all judges, results in a tendency never to ignore the value of legal reasoning, and often produces a psychological desire for certainty which can be easily found in the form of "binding authority" or logical argument from legal principles; (3) the occasional need to escape the agony of decision by relying on established rules; and (4) competing perceptions and strategies between judges and between the court and its constituents.[31] We can describe these limitations but we have found it extremely difficult to measure them. Third, even if we could assume that judicial decisions and opinion verbiage were unaffected by the gamesmanship and limitations suggested above, decisions reached and opinions written would still, at least occasionally, produce the mistaken impression that they were arrived at on the basis of personal predilection rather than precedent and legal reasoning. Two of the reasons for this appear to be: (1) the necessity of advocacy, that is, the need to persuade colleagues often turns the simplicity of opinion writing into special pleading, a tendency (stimulated by the inevitability of personal antagonisms) which leads to simplistic and overstated conclusions; and (2) the heavy workload and frequent demands for speedy decisions sometimes lead to the use of standard arguments to support conclusions reached not on the basis of predilection as they therefore appear, but on the basis of a complex calculus of legal reasoning.[32]

Clearly, answers to the substantive question—what variables are at work and what is their proportionate distribution—must be limited. So that the reader will not think that there are no conclusions in the study of the judicial decision, let us examine the variables. First, a brief word about approach. Methodological sophistication emerged with C. Herman Pritchett's seminal study, *The Roosevelt Court*,[33] in which he unveiled the technique of "inter-agreement matrix" construction to study bloc activity on the Court. Since then, many new (and some old) methods have been used to get at the elusive nature of the judicial decision: biography, psychoanalysis, content analysis, cumulative scaling, cost analysis, factor analysis, etc. And most available literature makes conclusions based on a particular method associated with the analysis of a particular variable.[34] In this study conclusions will be cased on variables rather than method.

Background Attributes. In many ways judges are very similar to each other. They are, in general, far better educated and of higher socioeconomic status than most other people, even than most other lawyers. This is particularly true for the U.S. Supreme Court where it has been observed that the typical justice

has invariably been white, generally Protestant with a penchant for high social status denomination, usually of ethnic stock originating in the British Isles, and born in comfortable circumstances in an urban or small town environment. In the earlier history of the Court, he very likely was born in the aristocratic or gentry class, while later he tended to come from the professionalized upper middle-class.[35]

Since judges are lawyers, they also share to at least some degree a common professional socialization experience. And Grossman observes that another socialization process begins when a judge first comes to the bench. This process functions, in turn, as an informal socialization process for future judges in that they see and imitate the career patterns of successful judicial candidates.[36] Regarding U.S. Supreme Court and state supreme court justices, for example, several background attributes are held in common: they are usually of the same party as the appointing authority; they usually have had considerable political experience; and they usually come from politically active families.[37]

Although it is possible to make these generalizations, there are also significant differences of background among judges. Naturally then, scholars have attempted to discover relationships between background and judicial behavior. These attempts have often been successful though sometimes the conclusions are statistically weak. Let us examine.

Before the era of empirical analysis of judicial decision-making behavior, it was widely accepted that appellate court judges with prior judicial experience (on a lower court), having been schooled in the conservative norms expected of judges, would be more likely than judges without prior experience to adhere to precedent.[38] The opposite appears to be the case. Judges with prior experience are more likely to abandon precedent than judges without prior experience, apparently because they have developed sufficient confidence to disregard precedent in order to achieve their policy objectives.[39] Judges from low socioeconomic status are also more likely than others to abandon precedent.[40] Party and religion also appear to be significant background variables. Democratic and Catholic judges are more likely than Republican and Protestant judges to vote for "liberal results," specifically, to vote to protect civil rights and criminal defendants, to favor government regulation of business, and to favor employees over employers.[41] More specifically, Democratic judges are more likely than Republican judges to vote for the administration agency in business-regulation cases, for the government in tax cases, for the tenant in landlord-tenant cases, for the consumer in consumer protection cases, for the claimant in unemployment compensation cases, for the employee in employee-injury cases, and for the defense in criminal cases.[42] In fact, in criminal cases, at least three background attributes and one general attitudinal variable are important: judges with prior experience as prosecutors, judges who are ABA members, and judges who are Protestants are more likely to vote for the prosecution than are judges without prosecutorial experience, non-ABA members, and Catholics. More generally, liberal judges (who rank high on "general liberalism" as measured by an attitude questionnaire) vote much more regularly for the defense in criminal cases than those who rank low on liberalism.[43]

The basic suggestion here is that certain backgrounds are conducive to the formation of certain attitudes or values which in turn affect decisional behavior; that there is a relationship between discrete backgrounds and judicial decision-making tendencies. This is not to say that judges are prisoners of their past but only that their values which determine, in part, their decisions have been shaped by life experiences.[44] It is true that some of the relationships cited above are statistically weak and that, in fact, some studies have found practically no explanatory power in background attributes. However, the hypothesis that background attributes are related to judicial decisions will not die. The reality probably is that background attributes influence and filter through the complex interactions between values, role perceptions, and bloc activity to produce a result that is not unassociated with the character of the attributes themselves.

FIGURE 3. JUSTICES AND VALUE SYSTEMS

	Freedom	Equality	New Dealism	Value System Description
Douglas	+	+	+	Liberal
Warren	+	+	+	Liberal
Goldberg	+	+	+	Liberal
Fortas	+	+	+	Liberal
Brennan	+	+	+	Liberal
Marshall	+	+	+	Liberal
Black	+	–	+	Populist
White	0	0	0	moderate
Stewart	0	0	0	moderate
Clark	–	–	+	New Dealer
Whittaker	–	–	–	Conservative
Frankfurter	–	–	–	Conservative
Harlan	–	–	–	Conservative
Blackmun	–	–	–	Conservative
Burger	–	–	–	Conservative

Legend: + supports the value
      – does not support the value
      0 neutral

Source: Harold J. Spaeth, *An Introduction to Supreme Court Decision Making* (San Francisco: Chandler, 1972), p. 68.

Values, Role Perceptions, and Bloc Activity. Many studies have now successfully associated the values (or attitudes or "policy preferences") of judges with their judicial decisions. To put it another way, values are revealed in the decisions judges make. It must be admitted, of course, that the cumulative scaling technique usually used to discern attitudinal dimensions cannot be used to prove that values cause decisions because there is no way to measure values independent of votes—we cannot conclude that values cause votes because we have defined values in terms of those same votes. But if the "values-cause-votes" hypothesis was invalid, the cumulative scaling studies would not have found the repeated issue-oriented voting they have, in fact, found.[45] Three clusters of values in particular have been found in scaling Supreme Court voting behavior for the years 1958-73: appropriately labeled "freedom," "equality," and "New Dealism."[46] By fitting the fifteen justices who served on the Court between 1958 and 1971 into this typology the value system descriptions shown on Figure 3 emerge. Again, this is not to say that values alone cause votes but only that:

based upon the assumption that all human behavior is goal oriented, and that individuals are continually faced with alternative courses of action, one may hypothesize that an individual will choose from among the alternatives available the one that he perceives best achieves his goals. The decisions an individual makes, then, will depend upon his personal value system—the set of beliefs, attitudes, and values that disposes him to behave in a certain fashion.[47]

However, when all is said and done, the judicial decision-making process is not that simple. The role perception of the judge as either an "activist" or "restraintist" (or something else) may be a significant intervening variable. "Activism" is difficult to describe because although it may, in fact, explain more judicial decisions than does "restraint," few judges will publicly admit to being activists. Activism, in short, indicates a desire to insert one's policy preferences into judicial decisions in order to achieve policy goals and a willingness to overturn the decisions of the political branches to accomplish that objective. However, for some judges, in some cases role demands may be stronger than policy preferences, or to put it differently, playing the proper role may be the highest of competing values. Judicial restraint, for example, posits that judges should refrain from making public policy. They should not address policy issues unless it is absolutely necessary to do so to dispose of a concrete case. If they must address policy issues they should frame them as narrowly as possible and never arrive at a rule which is broader than required to dispose of the case. They should always defer to the political branches of government (legislatures and executives) on subjective judgments concerning the wisdom or utility of legislation and administrative orders. They should, in short, stay out of the political thicket. It is true that restraint is practiced not only by those judges who truly are guided by the restraintist role demand and apply it generally and across the board, but also by those who are guided by policy preferences and apply it selectively in particular instances to promote their policy goals. But clearly, the often conflicting demands of policy preference and role have a lot to do with how judges decide, as the following account of Justice Wiley Rutledge's decision in *Colegrove v. Green*[48] illustrates.

Colegrove involved a suit to restrain Illinois from electing congressmen from grossly unequal districts. The Court's majority followed Justice Frankfurter's argument that the issue in question was one "of a peculiarly political nature and therefore not meet for judicial determination." In the majority's view, legislative apportionment was a "political question" to be dealt with by legislative bodies or administrative commissions. The Court, the majority reasoned, should remain aloof from political entanglements, should not allow itself to be perceived by the public as a policy maker (or else it would lose the one source of power it has—sustained public confidence in its antiseptic impartiality). In 1946 the Court was shorthanded. Justice Jackson was in Nuremberg and Justice Stone, recently deceased, had not yet been replaced. Of the remaining seven Justices, three (Black, Douglas, and Murphy) clearly favored intervention in the apportionment controversy. Three others (Frankfurter, Reed, and Burton) wanted to stay out of the "political thicket." Rutledge held the swing vote and an examination of his past decision-making behavior would have indicated a high value accorded to equality and hence a prediction that he would join those who wished to intervene in the apportionment controversy here. Rutledge changed his mind twice in the matter. At first, he agreed with Frankfurter that the Court should remain aloof especially since it could provide no remedy. The best it could do would be to invalidate the presently malapportioned system leaving Illinois with no choice but to elect congressmen at large across the state unless the state legislature or governor were to act before the next election. But then the high place Rutledge accorded to the value of equality, prevailed. He decided that in an electoral system where one district has eight times the population of another, the resulting discrimination necessarily deprives citizens of equal protection of the laws. Finally, however, Rutledge's role demand prevailed. He valued equality, but he also exhibited remarkable restraint when he felt restraint necessary in order to achieve a firm result; to preserve the image of symmetry, continuity, and certainty in the law; or to protect the Court's standing with the public. In *Colegrove*, he did not want to see a seven-man Court make such an important decision as to intervene in an apportionment controversy for the first time. He feared that a nine-man Court once restored, might well order a reargument and reverse the decision. Such a turn-about, he felt, would damage the Court. So in the end, he joined with the restraintists, Frankfurter, Reed, and Burton, to form a 4–3 majority against intervention. In the complex calculus of decision, role had prevailed over policy preference in this instance.[49]

In addition to values and role demands we must also inquire into the impact of bloc activity on the judicial decision. A "bloc," according to Schubert, "consists of three or more judges who manifest a relatively high degree of interagreement in their voting, whether in the majority or in dissent, over a period of at least a term."[50] Schubert identified and analyzed a "certiorari bloc" of Murphy, Rutledge, Black, and Douglas operating in the Supreme Court from 1943–49 which successfully pursued an objective of supporting claimants in Federal Employer's Liability Act cases. Schubert postulated that these four justices created a bloc with the deliberate objective of forcing upon the rest of the Court the consideration of an issue which the bloc wanted decided in a particular way. Assuming that:

the objective of the bloc was to maximize the number of decisions favorable to workmen's claims, game theory can prescribe how the bloc should behave rationally in order to accomplish this objective. Four Justices are adequate to grant certiorari, but not (normally) to decide cases on the merits. It is assumed that, during this period, the remaining five Justices had no fixed predisposition either toward or against the claimants. The only question in these cases is whether the trial court correctly evaluated evidence; the cases turn, in other words, on questions of fact rather than law. Typically, they fall into two categories: (a) the trial court directs a judgment for the defendant railroad on the ground that the evidence is insufficient for the case to go to a jury, or else the court directs a judgment for the defendant notwithstanding a jury verdict for the plaintiff; or (b) the trial judge enters a judgment for the plaintiff on the basis of a jury verdict. In either event, the decision of the trial court has been affirmed or reversed by a court of appeals, and either the plaintiff workman or the defendant railroad has petitioned the Supreme Court for certiorari.[51]

Now, the bloc of Murphy, Rutledge, Black, and Douglas needed only to pick up one additional favorable vote on the merits, and, assuming that there is an equal chance that any of the five uncommitted justices will vote either for or against a claimant if the court of appeals has disagreed with the trial court, the chances of the bloc picking up that vote should be 31/32, because the only permutation of the five uncommitted members on which the bloc could lose would be for all five to vote against the claimant. Thus, according to game theory, the bloc's pure strategy would be never to vote in favor of petitions filed by railroads, always to vote to grant certiorari in cases in which review is sought by workmen and in which an appellate court has reversed a judgment in favor of the plaintiff, and always to vote for the petitioner on the merits. If the bloc plays the game rationally, always following its pure strategy, the Court should decide 97 percent of the cases in favor of the claimants. Schubert found that, as a matter of fact, the payoff to the certiorari bloc on FELA cases from 1943 to 49 was 92 percent in cases in which the bloc adhered to its pure strategy.[52]

The construction of interagreement matrices to study bloc activity was, in fact, begun before Schubert's study of the certiorari bloc by C. Herman Pritchett in his seminal works, *The Roosevelt Court*[53] and *Civil Liberties and the Vinson Court.*[54] Pritchett discovered a "libertarian activist bloc" consisting of the same four justices as Schubert's certiorari bloc and operating during the same period. The libertarian activist bloc, perhaps the best known bloc within recent years, demonstrated an extremely high rate of interagreement in support of civil liberties issues. Pritchett found that while the average rate of support of the Court for these issues was 35 percent during the period, only five of the eleven different justices serving on the Court in the 1940s had averages above this mean. Specifically, the following individual rates of support were found: Murphy (100 percent), Rutledge (96 percent), Douglas (89 percent), Black (87 percent), and Frankfurter (61 percent). Pritchett's hypothesis was that decisions involving civil liberties issues are primarily influenced by the interaction of two factors: (1) "the direction and intensity of a Justice's libertarian sympathies, which will vary according to his weighing of the relative claims of liberty and order;" and (2) "the conception which the Justice holds of his judicial role and the obligations imposed on him by his judicial function."[55] Thus, he concludes, Murphy, Rutledge, Black, and Douglas were both libertarian and activist, while Frankfurter was libertarian in personal sympathies but a self-retraintist in judicial role. The other six justices, Pritchett labeled simply "less Libertarian."[56]

The pioneering bloc analyses of Schubert and Pritchett help suggest both the complexity of the judicial decision and the "gaming" that often transpires in the formation of a majority vote. More recent studies using even more advanced techniques suggest that the making of judicial decisions may be even more complex than even Schubert and Pritchett supposed. The cost model of Atkinson and Neuman is illustrative.[57] Regarding the bloc variable as well as others we have discussed, hypotheses for testing are today commonly generated from the careful examination of the private papers of judges. Atkinson and Neuman used such private papers to generate three plausible hypotheses of judicial behavior: (H_1) Supreme Court justices vote so as to protect the institutional stability of the Court; (H_2) Supreme Court justices vote so as to avoid isolation; and (H_3) Supreme Court justices vote so as to protect the integrity of their doctrinal commitments.[58] Using vote data collected for individual justices during four Court terms (1949-52), Atkinson and Neuman developed a "cost index" which revealed for any justice dissenting or concurring, the cost to him in terms of personal isolation and/or lost institutional stability. They found a good deal of consistency in voting behavior over the four terms and identified a "Truman bloc" (of Justices Vinson, Clark, Burton, and Minton, all Truman appointees) which voted almost invariably in accordance with the first hypothesis.

Although this approach has its shortcomings,[59] it is useful in helping to determine empirically which of various plausible hypotheses is most supported by the data for a given judge. As such, it not only helps to explain bloc voting, but also dramatizes the complex interplay of the at once conflicting and complementing variables of values, role perceptions, and bloc activity.

Finally, we must make a brief comment about the intellectual method (or mode of reasoning) a judge uses in arriving at a decision. Although there are, as yet, no aggregate data on this matter, studies of individual judges suggest the hypothesis that intellectual method varies with the value-content of the case before the judge. The intellectual method of Wiley Rutledge is again illustrative. For Rutledge, the premises of democracy logically entailed the expansion of the welfare state. At the same time, he insisted that for democracy to survive, the fundamental moral standards of human rights and freedoms had to be maintained. As he saw it, there was nothing in the Constitution which precluded the use of far-reaching public power, but that same Constitution, he believed, absolutely prohibited governmental intrusions into the private provinces of personal rights. The apparently competing values of security and freedom were not, however, incompatible in his mind. To support his views on socioeconomic issues, his intellectual method was pragmatic and based on a fundamental realism. On issues of personal freedom, however, his mode of reasoning was largely a priori and reflected an ethic and a humanism characteristic of natural law jurisprudence. We referred in chapter 2 to Cardozo's "complex brew," the judicial decision. We now understand that the ingredients (values, role perceptions, bloc activity) must be stirred with differing ladles of intellectual method.

The Fact/Value "Dichotomy." Today, few social scientists would disagree that the values of judges are among the crucial determinants of their decisions. But, clearly, the facts presented by a concrete case and the legal precedents related to those facts are also important determinants. Indeed, some studies show that as many as 8 of 10 decisions in unanimous cases can be predicted accurately using precedent alone as the independent variable, while values alone can predict no more than 1 of 3 decisions in unanimous cases.[60] It is true, of course, that the percentage of accurate predictions using values alone increases in nonunanimous cases, and generally nonunanimous cases are recognized as providing a better clue to judicial motivation because the unanimous decision is one in which either (1) the legal precedent is so clear that any exercise of judicial discretion is completely foreclosed, or (2) discretion was available but because the respective values of the judges were all so similar they all came to the same answer. Hence, nonunanimous decisions are usually used for decision-making analyses because, working with an identical set of facts, judges are coming to different conclusions, thus, there is some assurance that the result was influenced at least in part by values. Still, there remains a central problem: how to measure the relative weights of values and facts as they combine to produce the judicial decision.

Until recently, it was widely assumed that values and facts were dichotomous variables. That is, some studies emphasized the importance of facts and concluded that facts determined values; others emphasized values and concluded that values determined facts. Today, although it is difficult to generalize from one study, Werner Grunbaum's computer-based content analysis of *Williams v. Rhodes*[61] has led to a wholly different set of conclusions. (1) Both value and fact variables are significant in the judicial decision-making process. (2) However, they are not dichotomous variables; they are complementary and associative, that is, there is no evidence indicating either that facts determine values or that values determine facts. Rather, the relation between fact and value variables is one in which facts influence values and values influence the perception of facts. In other words, the two variables are associated and neither variable alone accounts for the voting outcome. (3) The finding noted above helps to explain why facts alone appear to frequently predict decisions. The facts of a case fix its position on the judge's value scale and it is this position which determines his vote. Facts alone appear to predict outcome because when a judge's values remain stable over a long period of time he will decide cases of similar factual content similarly. But it is not the facts alone that determine the outcome, it is the association of facts with the judge's previous typical values.[62]

5

LAWYERS AND LEGAL STYLE

THE LEGAL PROFESSION

Lawyers are not only important participants in the judicial process but also constitute a plurality in policy-making bodies of all sorts. They bring with them to these policy-making arenas (judicial and nonjudicial) a distinctive style which sets narrow limits on the data they consider and on the remedies they propose. The origins of this style are to be found in the professional organization, training, and socialization of the bar.

Origins of the Bar.   As was pointed out in chapter 2, the appearance of a professional class of lawyers did not occur until the mature phase of the law's development. In Anglo-American legal history the ordinary person could adequately represent himself in court up until about the middle of the twelfth century when the growing body of law and the growing complexity of legal procedure necessitated the assistance of someone trained in the style of technical pleading. At first, anyone could act as a *responsalis,* a person appointed by a litigant to do his technical pleading. By the early thirteenth century, however, both technical pleading and the demands of oral argument required a special skill which resulted in the evolution of a recognized profession of lawyers. During the reign of Henry III (1216-72) a group of "narrators," as they were called, emerged to speak for litigants in the king's courts and to play the role of advocate. At the same time the king required lawyers of his own to represent his interests in court. Thus, he appointed *servientes regis,* "sergeants of the king" to handle his legal business. By the end of the thirteenth century these *servientes regis* were permitted to serve as counsel for private litigants when not busy with the king's litigation, and they replaced the narrators. Perhaps most precisely we can identify the institution of a formal legal profession with an edict issued by Edward I in 1292. This edict placed the education of lawyers in the hands of the common pleas courts which could then choose those "attorneys and learners" who alone would be permitted to practice before the court. Thus began the monopoly of legal business by the legal profession.[1]

Legal Training and Education. The impact of originally charging the courts with legal education cannot be exaggerated. It meant that lawyer taught lawyer while each learned from court processes. The result was that English (and ultimately American) law drew from its own resources, became insular, isolated from the influences of Roman and ecclesiastical law. Students would sit at an observation bench (called "the crib") and take notes. Sometimes they were permitted to ask questions during the course of the trial. The custom of lawyers and law students living and learning together during terms of court gave rise to the unique English institution of the "Inns of Court" in which the tradition of the common law was taught. Lincoln's Inn, the first of these institutions, was created during the reign of Edward I (1272–1307) to be followed by about a dozen others.[2] In the United States this tradition never took hold. During colonial times and continuing through a large part of the nineteenth century, "law students" were not necessarily college graduates but persons who studied the law while working in the office of an established lawyer known as the "preceptor." There was practically no type of formal legal education prior to the Civil War. Generally, law was not taught by established universities because it was generally thought to be "too vulgar a subject" for scholarly pursuit. There were a few independent law schools (like the old Litchfield Law School) where students read treaties and listened to lectures, but such training was still followed by an apprenticeship of some sort before the lawyer asked a court for admission to the bar. The adoption of the case method at Harvard and a few other universities after the Civil War made the study of law "scientific" and thus acceptable as a subject of instruction in prestigious schools. In this century university-affiliated legal education has become the nearly exclusive mode of legal training. In 1900 the American Association of Law Schools (AALS) was founded with the assistance of the American Bar

Association as an accrediting body to upgrade the quality of legal instruction. Today, in most states, a prospective lawyer must graduate from a three-year law school and then pass a standardized bar examination in order to practice law.[3]

Bar Associations. Bar associations were founded originally on the local level to help combat municipal corruption. The American Bar Association was founded in 1878 principally in order to work for improvement in the quality of legal training. Most lawyers belonged to neither local associations nor the ABA during these early years. By the early twentieth century, however, politically-minded lawyers began to realize that if they were to have any political clout as a group they would have to be better organized. The idea of making bar association membership compulsory in order to practice in a given state became the principal agenda item of the American Judicature Society which was founded by Herbert Harley in 1913. Rather than saddling such compulsory membership with the politically pejorative label, "closed shop," the Society designated its objective, the "integrated bar." Today, integrated bars exist in slightly over half the states and both integrated and voluntary bar associations have worked to improve the quality of legal education and to increase the availability of legal services to the public. They have also pursued more nearly self-serving goals, however, such as restricting entry into the profession so that lawyers would not have to compete too strenuously for the available legal work.[4]

Lawyers and the Administration of Justice. Lawyers alone may practice law in American courts and lawyers alone are permitted to transact out-of-court legal business. Hence, lawyers as a group are central to the administration of justice in the United States. On the other hand, most lawyers are not directly involved in the making of public policy. Approximately half of the 325,000 lawyers in the United States are involved in solo, private practice. They write contracts and wills for clients, give advice on tax matters, arrange for the sale of property and handle civil and criminal litigation for private persons. Others perform similar tasks as members of a partnership or of large firms though they are here employed more commonly as specialists. Still others are employed as "house counsel" where they work for one corporate employer. As private lawyers all of the above practitioners are key participants in the administration of justice but as counselors and advocates they are only rarely consciou of the policy implications of their work. Outside the judicial arena they participate in politics only sporadically (though more frequently than nonlawyers).

This description of the nonpolitical, routine tasks of lawyers is a bit misleading, however. Although most lawyers are not directly involved in the making of public policy, policy-making councils (legislative and administrative) on both the national and state levels are dominated by lawyers. There are currently eighteen thousand lawyers employed in one capacity or another by the national government and probably a figure approaching ten times that many are employed by the states. From the beginning of the American republic, political leadership has been preempted by lawyers. De Tocqueville considered lawyers to be an intellectual elite exercising a preponderant influence in the American polity, and with good reason. Twenty-five of the fifty-six signers of the Declaration of Independence were lawyers, as were thirty-three of the fifty-five framers of the Constitution.[5] A substantial majority of our presidents and secretaries of state have been lawyers, and lawyers have constituted a plurality of our members of Congress and of our state's governors from the beginning. Today, lawyers remain ubiquitous in policy-making councils, legislative, executive, and judicial. Even in the nonjudicial arenas, they are almost always a plurality. The importance of lawyers not only to the formal administration of justice but also to the making of public policy generally is a social fact. For generations they have come in for sharp criticism but only recently have they been subjected to careful, empirical analysis.

LEGAL STYLE[6]

It has long been argued that lawyers are "a hidebound lot who worship the past and are constantly searching for means to delay and obstruct the forces of social progress."[6] Although a strong case can be made to the contrary—that lawyers have helped adapt the law to changing social needs and have helped improve judicial administration as well,[7] only recently has social science begun to empirically examine the extent of political participation by lawyers[8] and the impact of their allegedly conservative bias on policy making. Unfortunately, most of these studies are either too narrowly framed or are otherwise conceived in such a way as to miss the main point to be analyzed about lawyer–policy makers. For example,

Dyer's study of state legislative voting behavior on no-fault insurance bills successfully shows that lawyers in state legislatures are less likely to support no-fault proposals that would affect the amount of available legal business than are nonlawyers.[10] But this finding indicates only that lawyer-legislators vote to support the interests of the legal profession, not that lawyers exhibit a conservative bias in their legislative voting generally. Further, the legislative voting behavior of lawyer-legislators may be the least significant indicator of their impact on policy outputs. As Derge has suggested (and Dyer appears to agree), lawyers occupy key leadership positions in legislative bodies and have opportunities to influence policy in the "private" arenas of legislative decision making in ways that do not show up in public roll call votes.[11] The same can undoubtedly be said for the role of lawyers in the similarly, relatively private administrative arenas of policy making. Another study which attempts to get at the allegedly conservative bias of lawyer-legislators is that of Eulau and Sprague which finds, to the contrary, that lawyer-legislators have a slightly more liberal voting record than their nonlawyer peers.[12] A recent study by McIntosh and Stanga attempts to explain this unexpected finding, in part, by illustrating that Democratic lawyers participate in politics more regularly than Republicans and hence the "conservative bias associated with lawyers is counterbalanced by the tendency of Democratic lawyers to be more active politically. . . ."[13]

Again, both of these studies miss the main point. Democratic lawyers may be more liberal than Republican lawyers but both are lawyers and both are constrained by their legal training and frame of mind. It is their approach to policy making and the bag and baggage they take with them that sets them apart from other policy makers. Moreover, the constraints of the legal style manifest themselves long before final votes are taken (in legislative bodies) and long before rules are announced (by administrative bodies). By the time the lawyer–policy maker acts to formalize the final decision, the policy has already been made. The "legal style" thesis we will explore in this section is that: (1) lawyers, because of the demands of legal theory and by virtue of their training and professional socialization, approach policy making with a distinctive style which sets narrow limits on the data they consider and on the remedies they propose; and (2) the ubiquity of lawyers in the policy process coupled with the tendency of other policy makers to defer to them even on matters outside their realm of expertise, makes the legal style a principal determinant of incremental process and substance in policy making.

Origins—Legal Theory and Training. Although legal theorists recognized early that any attempt to construct a legal system analogous to Euclidean geometry was doomed to failure, they have never given up their tendency to look constantly inward for consistency and symmetry in any legal framework they posit. And this tendency exists to at least some degree regardless of what the theorist perceives to be the source or motive force of law. Whether the theorist defines law with an exaggerated emphasis on "a body of rules in force" or with an exaggerated emphasis on "a type of machinery for accommodating conflicting interests," he tends to argue that the fundamental social interest to be protected by any legal system is the need for uniformity and impartiality in the law itself. The resulting prescription is for symmetrical development and, consequently, for adherence to precedent. To be sure, some theorists recognize that symmetrical development may be bought at too high a price, especially when it comes into conflict with the social interest served by equity and fairness or other elements of social welfare, but they are in the minority. Even though most legal theorists may admit to the existence of such apparent paradoxes as stability versus change in legal development (just as they admit to the existence of the paradox between fixity and discretion in judicial method), they tend to believe that the fundamental guide to the discovery of the law and to the solution of the paradox is the syllogism. To a degree, they may tend to be persuaded by Justice Holmes's suggestion that the life of the law is to be found in experience not logic. But, on balance, they cannot break free from the belief that the rules of formal logic are indispensable to the legal scholar, the jurist, and the lawyer alike, not only as a means for exposing the fallacies of an argument but also as a means for systematizing the law by facilitating the discovery of the real source of legal rules.

This is not to argue that all legal theorists conceive of law as a mere collection of detailed rules and deny its inherent power of growth and adaptation to changed circumstnaces. Indeed, to defend the proposition that the law is capable of growth, some theorists cite the importance in legal development of the theory of the "logical plenitude of law"—the notion that a judge cannot refuse to decide a case on the ground that there is no precise authority in point. But when there is no authority in point, what determines the judge's decision? Most theorists argue that he will rely on custom, analogy, textbooks, or some mix of the three. And herein lies the point. All three of these sources have a still narrowing, exclusionary effect on the materials considered and the results produced. The search remains, even without the demands of rigorous logic, a search for systematic order, for the *ratio legis* behind the law. The resulting view of the legal process is one of a closed system characterized by internal consistency and certainty, systematically expounded. Materials from outside the system, even if relevant, are excluded unless through the "proper use of analogy" they can be internalized. And the determination of the "proper use of analogy" is itself made by a legal construct requiring the "relative importance of the resemblances and the unimportance of the differences between the two things." In short, the only advantage gained by the proper use of analogy is to enable the law to deal with new situations by adopting a rule which can be placed in a coherent relation with rules already established.[14] Again, consistency and symmetry are the dominant determinants of development.

Granted, there are those legal theorists who see some opportunity for extraneous input. Usually, such inputs are characterized as resulting from an "inarticulate major premise" by which is meant a "social picture" or a body of political or ethical ideals which give direction to the law. This is precisely what Justice Holmes meant by "the felt necessities of the times" and "intuitions of public policy." Clearly, as we have seen, the assumption that such considerations do influence the evolution of law was the central contribution of the legal realists in the law schools and the antecedent of judicial behavioralism in political science. But, on balance, most legal theorists argue that even when there is no precise authority in point, logical extension, even if from general principles, is a more important determinant of legal development than policy preferences.

It may be a bit unfair (not to mention inaccurate) to characterize all legal theory as fixed within the boundaries imposed by the demands of symmetrical development and the restrictions of legal reasoning. To be sure, there are those scholars who emphasize the law's fluidity and the "reasonable elasticity" which accompanies the application of legal rules. We are not so much concerned here with the scholar's view of the law as with the lawyer's view. The lawyer acquires his view from his legal training where the narrower view of the law prevails and the law student is taught that the key to professional success depends on the acquisition and development of analytical reasoning skills. The origins of the legal style in policy making can be thus traced back at least as far as to the nature of legal training. Indeed, it may go back even further to the screening of law school applicants and admission of those whose Law School Admission Test performance indicates a high probability that they possess sufficient analytical capacity to endure the rigors of legal training.

The criticism of legal education as being contracted, illiberal, and non-normative is not particularly new. It goes back at least as far as Woodrow Wilson's observation that the study of the law sharpens the mind by narrowing it. In recent years, however, Nader-type critics have accused legal education of irrelevance. According to these critics legal education is a "three-year excursus through legal minutiae, embraced by wooden logic."[15] It is a "process of engineering the law student into corridor thinking and largely non-normative evaluation" in which the professors "take delight in crushing egos in order to acculturate the students to what they call 'legal reasoning' or 'thinking like a lawyer.' The process is a highly sophisticated form of mind control that trades off breadth of vision . . . for freedom to roam in an intellectual cage."[16] It is usually then argued that pedagogical form perpetuates the status quo in pedagogical content so that the law student may take courses in estate planning but not in environmental planning, in collapsible corporations but not in collapsing tenements, in creditors' rights but not in debtors' remedies. The alleged result is that the law student emerges from his training without that cultivated sense of injustice which marked the great works of Pound and Frank and Llewellyn.[17]

We must admit that the latter part of this argument may now be a moot point, given the recent and rapid emergence of numerous "soft law" courses in most American law schools. Even a cursory perusal of current catalogs indicates a regular inclusion of such courses as Law and Poverty, Environmental Law, Consumer Protection Law, Urban Renewal Law, and Legal Problems of the American Indian, not to mention a broadening opportunity for "clinical courses" for credit. Thus it would be difficult to continue to aver that public policy is rarely the law school's concern. It may now be that legal education produces lawyers who are keenly sensitive to social problems and eager to use their specialized knowledge to formulate solutions.

We must be careful not to assume that changes in curricula content and a broadening of legal forums have been necessarily produced by or even accompanied by a broadening of legal form. Indeed, our argument is that even the "new lawyer," the lawyer with a cultivated sense of injustice, is just as limited, just as restricted in his approach to problem solving as the old lawyer. The law schools, regardless of the courses they offer, still consider their primary objective to be the imparting of analytical skills.

The law students' time is still taken up with making fine distinctions between law and fact, between governing facts and incidental ones, between *ratio decidendi* and *obiter dicta,* and between principles, standards, concepts, and rules. With these skills, the law student can usually provide a legal solution to a legal problem (as presented in a case book), but he is not necessarily equipped to devise new remedies when none exist. Even if he develops a remedy he is inclined to conceal the change or alteration in the law by the use of a legal fiction. In fact, the lawyers' need for the fiction is a perfect example of his handicap as a policy maker. It is not that he intends to deceive. It is simply the lawyer's tendency to use established devices that have worked well rather than to risk innovation. The point is that although the law student has been given more to think about he has not been given more to think with. He is still compelled to "think like a lawyer," which means that he continues to be confined by the world of the precedent, the syllogism, the analogy, and the fiction. Just as the introduction of the Brandeis brief liberalized the rules of evidence, the introduction of policy-oriented courses has liberalized the law school curriculum. But the new course content, just like the social science data allowed by the acceptance of the Brandeis brief, means only that the lawyer's substantive world is broadened while his style of thought remains narrow. This breadth of substance and narrowness of thought, and in turn, a narrowness in policy-making style is found throughout public policy.

A brief note must be entered here before we consider the impact of legal style on environmental policy making as an example of our thesis. The argument of this section on "legal style" is that lawyers approach policy making with a distinctive style whether they are working in a judicial or a nonjudicial arena. This thesis is particularly easy to illustrate for the judicial arena because the common law approach within a judicial review context colors American policy making with a legalistic cast, as pointed out long ago by de Tocqueville. But the thesis extends beyond the judicial arena to legislative and administrative policy-making councils as we will see at the end of our environmental policy example. The lawyer is present in these nonjudicial arenas in which his knowledge and skills are not those most relevant to the problem and his approaches do dominate policy making there nevertheless. He is deferred to not because he has subject matter expertise but, merely, because he is a lawyer. Relatively little research has been done on the role of lawyers in nonjudicial arenas. Letwin's study of the evolution and administration of the Sherman Antitrust

Act, probably the best available study, shows lawyers interacting with economists to guide the decision toward a legalistically oriented result. And those who have observed the U.S. Congress in action have undoubtedly noticed the pervasiveness of the common law style in its policy making: the adversary nature not only of hearings but also of floor debates, the tendency to ignore unrepresented interests (like the tendency of courts not to search beyond that which is presented to them by opposing counsel), congressional committee use of "out-of-court" settlement by the affected special interests, etc. Environmental litigation provides a useful illustration of the legal style thesis.

Environmental Policy as an Example. In chapter 8 we will examine the utility of the judicial process in solving policy problems and we will use environmental defense policy as one example. Let us use environmental policy as an example here of the legal style in policy making.

Prior to the 1960s there was little general interest in environmental protection. Attempts to clean up the environment and prevent its continued pollution through judicial, legislative, and administrative remedies began as the ranks of environmentalists swelled in the mid-1960s. Although a relatively new policy area, environmental defense has been approached in the traditional manner: the revival and application of ancient common law doctrines in the courts and deference to legal styles of reasoning and legal modes of planning in the legislative and administrative forums. The result has been a patchwork quilt of remedies, limited in scope and often conflicting in substance.

Environmental litigation has been generally of two types: the citizen lawsuit against private polluters seeking damages and injunctive relief, and the citizen lawsuit against public agencies and officials seeking review of official action or inaction. This litigation has been characterized by the employment of old and narrow legal tools, frustrated by fine distinctions between competing points of law, and resolved by applying time-tested standards of "balance" and "reasonableness." In short, the struggle between environmentalists and alleged polluters has been fought out within the conceptual limits imposed by either the distinctions between competing property rights or the notion of public encroachment upon private interests.

Actions against private polluters have been grounded usually on the ancient concepts of nuisance or trespass. The common law concept of nuisance has been the principal tool. For example, if B's home air conditioner produces an unusually loud noise causing A, an adjoining homeowner, great discomfort, a court can compensate A with money damages. Analogously, if a factory emits a substance into the air which damages A's property, A may be awarded damages. In each instance, if A can show that the legal remedy is inadequate, the court can enjoin B from continuation of his conduct. In other words, in each instance the pollution caused is a "nuisance" and can be legally banned.[18]

There are, however, a number of obstacles to successful actions in nuisance, some involving general legal reasoning and others legal technicalities. Generally, the plaintiff's problem has been to combat the "two-edged sword" argument and to end up on the prevailing side in "balancing the equities" tests. As pointed out in *Roberts v. C. F. Adams and Son*[19] the law of private nuisance is a "definition of the dividing line between the right of any owner to use his property as he so desires and the recognition of that right in another." Courts will usually pay lip service to the landowner's right to a pollution-free environment but will nevertheless recognize a right to do at least some polluting. The question then becomes one of "balancing the equities," and courts have been especially impressed by the need to balance the rights of the alleged polluter against the rights of the would-be private pollution controller when the controller is asking for an injunction instead of, or in addition to, money damages.[20]

The pollution controller may also run up against two other legal niceties: the technical distinction between public and private nuisances, and that magical concept of property law, "prescriptive rights." In the first instance, the controller must show that the pollution affects only one individual or several but is not common to the general public. If it is common to the general public, he must show that his injury is different in kind, not just degree, from that suffered by the general public. Otherwise, there is no right of action in the individual and the pollution can be abated only by an action instituted in the name of the state or its officials. In the second instance, the doctrine of prescriptive rights allows a polluter's wrongdoing, if it has continued for some time, to "ripen" (another both flexible and limiting concept) into a judicially protected right.[21] Krier, for example, has cited an instance in which a court was willing to go a long way to enjoin a plant from operating as long as it polluted the air, but it held that a second plant owned by the same defendant could continue to operate because the statute of limitations had run out and the defendant had thereby obtained a prescriptive right to its operation.[22] The doctrine of prescriptive rights has been characterized as "rewarding wrongdoers who are patient, persistent, and non-reforming."[23]

Actions in trespass are sometimes perceived by the private pollution controller as more suitable than actions in nuisance because he can avoid some of the legal obstacles noted above. He is, of course, continuing to play the game of legal strategies himself and can be easily caught in the crossfire of legalisms. He realizes on the one hand that by bringing an action in trespass he can usually avoid the vexatious problem of proving personal damage, and usually statutes of limitations are longer for trespass actions than for nuisance actions. On the other hand, however, he is commonly confronted with the legal fact that the trespass has occurred over a long period of time and has thus created a prescriptive right in the wrongdoer. At that point, he is forced to fall back on the tactics of arguing a public nuisance, against which a prescriptive right cannot legally "ripen." But if he attempts this maneuver he is back in the box of having to show that the public nuisance has produced special injury different in kind to him in order to bring the action. By choosing to deal with pollution control with legal strategy, the would-be pollution controller has a choice only of little boxes.

Lawsuits against administrative agencies and officers have relied upon and been frustrated by the same kinds of legal technicalities as have suits against private polluters. The most frequently employed means of seeking review of official action or inaction are suits for declaratory judgment or injunctive relief filed in a federal district court. The ancient common law writ of mandamus is also sometimes useful. Each of these remedies can be denied, however, if the court, applying the balancing test, finds that the injury to the public from granting the remedy outweighs its value to the plaintiff. Further, in the case of mandamus actions, the plaintiff is likely to be successful only if he can convince the court that the function to be performed is a "ministerial" and not a "discretionary" one. As Krier has noted, a court would probably order an agency to publish all of its pollution regulations. However, if the function is defined as discretionary, the results are far less predictable. The court would probably order the agency only to exercise its discretion.[24]

The most vexing problem for the citizen or environmental association in actions against public officials is the problem of "standing," "the most amorphous concept in the entire domain of the public law." Standing is a particularly significant barrier to environmental litigation in the federal courts. Suppose, for example, that a taxpayer wishes to protest a federal spending program allegedly harmful to the environment. A long line of cases from *Frothingham v. Mellon*[25] through *Flast v. Cohen*,[26] make it clear that the taxpayer must rely on a specific constitutional limitation on spending. Since there is no specific provision protecting the environment, it seems unlikely that he will be successful. It has been suggested, of course, by those who enjoy the game of legal ploys, that the Ninth Amendment grants every person a constitutional right to an environment free from pollution. To date, this argument has not gained judicial approval.[27] In *Sierra Club v. Hickel*,[28] in which the environmental association sought to enjoin the construction by Walt Disney Productions of a ski development in the Sequoia National Forest, the Supreme Court denied standing because it could find no adversary position established between the association and the secretary of interior.

In summary, environmentalists seeking action against both private polluters and public officials have either chosen or been forced to play the game of exchanging legal strategems. They have usually been hampered by jurisdictional, standing, or proof problems, and even when successful, they have found the applicable legal doctrines themselves too narrow. Increasingly, they are exhuming dead concepts, such as the public trust doctrine, to aid their cause. Although some of these concepts possess a broader potential, their utility is yet to be demonstrated.

Legislative and administrative approaches to environmental policy making, although they have grown and proliferated on both the national and state level in recent years, are also hampered by legal limitations and the usual deference to the lawyer's view of the planning stage.

On the state level, environmental action is predicated on the police power which authorizes the government to take such action as is reasonably necessary for the protection of the health, safety, morals, or welfare of its citizens. Even here, however, the test of reasonableness is paramount. Can a state, for example, pass legislation prohibiting excavation below the water level and imposing a duty on landowners to refill any excavation then below that level? The answer is in the affirmative only if it is shown that the interests of the public require the legislation and that the means are reasonably necessary for the accomplishment of the purpose. The courts must also decide whether the regulation, although an otherwise valid use of the police power, goes so far as to become "a taking" which constitutionally requires compensation.

The environmental effort on the national level has culminated in the passage of the National Environmental Policy Act of 1969, the creation of the Council on Environmental Quality, and the Environmental Protection Agency. While these accomplishments are aimed at "creating and maintaining conditions under which man and nature can exist in productive harmony," they have not been unmarked by the limits of legal style. In the first place, lawyers, who are generally inexpert in chemistry, biology, and physiology, are ill-equipped to make policy in an area which is inherently scientific, yet they have been deferred to. They have applied their penchant for the syllogism to reason that since pollution does not respect political boundaries such as state lines, uniform national standards should be the objective. Thus they have produced policies which disregard such imaginative possible solutions as the creation of pollution free areas. J. H. Dales has argued that uniform standards mean simply that no area will be clean. Therefore, the policy should be the creation of relatively clean areas and relatively polluted ones among which people could choose based on their individual judgment of personal needs.[29] At the same time, however, the environmental lawyer, though he prefers uniform standards, has opposed central coordination of policy. This is because he prefers having as many forums as possible to press his claims. He reasons that the more agencies involved in the process, the greater the likelihood that one of them will respond as he desires. The result has been a nightmare of overlapping jurisdictions and a more difficult time for environmental associations whose resources are too meager for the more diffused effort required.[30]

Summary. Lawyers commonly constitute a plurality in policy-making bodies of all sorts. They bring with them to these councils an approach to fact finding and policy planning which is characterized by the tendency to exclude information from consideration and to circumscribe possible solutions to problems with legal biases for consistency, symmetry, and stability. Rules of evidence and judicial notice serve to exclude much from the basis of court-made policy. Administrative and legislative procedures serve the same purpose for administrative hearing officers and legislators. Such exclusionary procedures were originally developed by the courts with reference to concrete cases in order to simplify the making of decisions. Indeed, most legal formalisms are attributable to the professional lawyer's tendency to multiply the rules of the judicial duel.[31] The carryover of these formalisms into the broader sphere of policy making also simplifies the making of decisions, but the appropriateness and costs of using such procedures are rarely considered by the lawyer-policy maker. Exclusionary procedures, for example, often define away many policy alternatives. Demands for symmetry and stability, similarly, often limit policy change to those alternatives which can be placed in a consistent and coherent relation with previous or existing policies. The lawyer–policy maker is forever fooling around with legal gadgetry. He includes and excludes information and policy alternatives with legal rituals. He devises then evades the legal fiction. He broadens and narrows the scope of participation in policy making with battles over standing. He exhumes ancient concepts such as nuisance and trespass and applies them adeptly to achieve limited objectives. His ploys seldom result in more than the skillful manipulation of legal minutiae for limited benefits. Even if successful, the policy change is usually temporal, lasting only until modified by another narrow but tangential legal thrust from some other quarter. Given the ubiquity of lawyers in the policy process, the primacy of lawyers in policy areas outside their expertise, and the deference to lawyers by other policy makers, the legal style in policy making (perhaps as much as pluralism itself) makes the policy process an incremental one and determines the content of policy.

6

CRIMINAL JUSTICE POLICY

THE FLOW OF CRIMINAL CASES

Despite the efforts of the FBI to collect data on the incidence of crime in the United States, we know relatively little about it. The Uniform Crime Reports (UCRs) compiled and published on an annual basis by the FBI are the only authoritative U.S. crime statistics. Although based on voluntary reports of police agencies, the UCRs usually cover about ninety-two percent of the population. Nevertheless, these statistics rarely provide either a complete or an accurate accounting of the problem of crime. One reason for the incomplete accounting is that much crime goes unreported. The best current estimate is that every year as many as fifty percent of all major crimes (that is, those that the UCRs include, such as murder, forcible rape, robbery, burglary, auto theft, etc.) go wholly unreported by the victim. Further, the FBI does not even attempt to compile statistics on "white collar crimes" such as tax fraud and price fixing. One reason for the innacurate accounting is the filing of false reports such as those alleging a burglary in order to defraud an insurance company. Another reason is that police chiefs occasionally file inaccurate reports intentionally: either reports that falsely exaggerate the incidence of crime in order to bolster their requests for more manpower and equipment or reports that are falsely rosy in order to create an image for themselves as heroic crime fighters. Nevertheless, we do know enough about crime to make the following statements: (1) during the decade of the 1960s while the population of the United States rose only thirteen percent, the incidence of reported major crime alone rose by one hundred and fifty percent; (2) in the instances of reported crime, an arrest of a suspect is made in only twenty-five percent of the cases and a conviction is ultimately obtained in only half of those cases where an arrest is made; (3) the rising crime rate and resulting backlog of criminal cases has impacted harmfully on the allocation of justice as evidenced by the fact that among those suspects ultimately convicted and sentenced about eighty percent are never proved guilty; rather, their sentences are based on "plea bargaining" in which the suspect pleads guilty to a lesser charge in exchange for a lighter sentence or some other benefit; and (4) those persons who do serve time in corrections facilities show few signs of being rehabilitated as evidenced by the fact that sixty-seven percent of those who are released utlimately return to a life of crime.[1] For these and other reasons the criminal justice shuttle system warrants scholarly attention.

In a strictly formal and traditional sense, we can describe the flow of cases in the criminal justice system as a four-stage process: arrest, arraignment, negotiation and/or trial, and sentencing. Arrests are usually made by police officers who exercise a great deal of discretion in the process. In some instances (typically family disputes and cases of social gambling), no arrest is made even though a crime has been committed. No arrest is made either because the officer's guess is that a conviction in court would be difficult to obtain or because the officer thinks a warning and a lecture are more appropriate. In other instances (typically cases of drunkenness and prostitution), arrests are made but with no intent to prosecute. The real reasons for such arrests are usually merely to harass and remove "undesirables" from the streets. If an arrest is made with an intent to prosecute, the next stage is arraignment, at which the defendant is charged, is given an opportunity to make a plea, and the amount of bail under which he may go free until subsequent proceedings is established. The arraignment is usually preceded by a "preliminary hearing" to determine probable cause for holding a suspect in felony cases. The next stage is that of negotiation between the prosecutor and the defendant (or his attorney) which may include plea bargaining. Most criminal cases are settled at this stage without trial. If the case does go to trial the prosecution usually wins because the prosecutor will already have sought to compromise through negotiation in those cases in which he is not virtually certain of winning a conviction. Finally, after conviction, sentence is passed by the judge. Although the final decision is his, the judge is usually presented with a recommendation by the prosecutor (which he commonly accepts). The court may also be aided by a "presentencing investigation report" filed by a social worker or probation officer. In the end, however, the judges have as much discretion in their sentencing decisions as do the police in their decisions to arrest or not to arrest and the prosecutors in their decisions to negotiate or to go to trial.[2]

In reality, few cases flow smoothly through the process as described above. What Judge Macklin Fleming calls "sidetracking" (maneuvers diverting the inquiry into collateral issues) and "mainlining" (maneuvers which deliberately delay, for example, fights over jury selection, production of evidence, custodial facilities, etc.)[3] serve to complicate and fragment the process. Indeed, a fragmented process is nearly unavoidable. The existence of parallel court systems produces "vertical fragmentation" in criminal justice policy while the complexities of the police-court-corrections relationship produce "horizontal fragmentation." The impact of intergovernmental (vertical) and interagency (horizontal) fragmentation has only recently been subjected to empirical analysis. The former has grown in importance since the middle 1960s as the national courts, national laws, and national agencies have increasingly come to deal with state and local law enforcement problems. And one study in particular has shown that the more national programs impose on state and local autonomy (that is, as they move from merely providing hardware, to providing training, to requiring consolidation of law enforcement structures) the more susceptible they are to distortion if not complete resistance.[4] Fragmentation of policy inevitably results because police, court, and corrections agencies have differing perceptions of crime and adopt conflicting strategies for dealing with it, and the horizontal linkages between these agencies are disjointed at best.[5] Again, fragmentation is inevitable. Let us examine the flow of cases in the criminal justice process in light of these fragmenting forces.

INTERAGENCY EXCHANGE

Criminal justice policy making takes place within what the social scientist would label a "nonsystem." Analytically, the police-courts-corrections complex is probably best described as no more than an arena in which criminal justice participants, each with differing perceptions of crime and corrections, play out their roles in accordance with unscrutinized values and inarticulate objectives. In short, program development and policy planning in the criminal justice area are incremental and fragmented. Although a nonsystem, the police-courts-corrections complex does have one inescapable systems characteristic—interdependence. Although each structure has analytically distinct functions, what each does has a distinct, though analytically blurred, effect on the others. The suspect is apprehended by the police, prosecuted, acquitted or convicted, and sentenced by the courts, and removed, punished, and/or rehabilitated by correctional agencies. Inherent in this separation of functions are disjointed linkages between agencies and conflicting agency strategies which produce fragmentation of both process and policy.

The analytical framework we will use to study these agencies and their roles in the criminal justice process is one of "interorganizational exchange" as developed by William M. Evan[6] and as applied to the analysis of the decision-making behavior of prosecutors by George F. Cole.[7] This framework depicts the legal process as an institutionalized setting (analogous to a market) in which participants (police, prosecutors, defense attorneys, judges, corrections officials, probation and parole officers) occupy "boundary-spanning" roles. The participants exchange cues, recommendations, refusals, bargains, threats, and resources, thus affecting the achievement of goals. The "exchange" implies both cooperation among agencies (because they are interdependent subunits) and competition among agencies (because their power depends largely upon their ability to create favorable clientele relationships in an arena of scarce resources). Cole's exploratory study of the King County (Seattle) Prosecutor's Office demonstrates that most criminal justice decisions result from some type of exchange relationship.[8]

FIGURE 4. THE CRIMINAL JUSTICE EXCHANGE SYSTEM

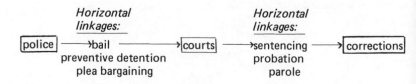

Disjointed Linkages between Agencies. The criminal justice process is ordinarily represented not as a set of random actions but as an orderly progression of events[9]—a continuum, if you will, linked by procedural fixations as suggested by figure 4.

The difficulty is that the three agencies not only have differing conceptions of the horizontal linkages but make procedural decisions regarding the linkages with little or no attention to the impact of those decisions on the functions of the other agencies, except in those instances in which they are consciously attempting to influence the others. Further, the traditional linkages between the police and the courts—bail, preventive detention, and plea bargaining—and the traditional linkages between the courts and corrections—probation, sentencing, and parole—are both ill-defined and in transition. In addition, the growing number of impact/compliance studies suggest, among the other things dealt with below, that one of the impacts of the "due process revolution" in the courts has been the increased use of plea bargaining by the prosecution.

The due process revolution can be said to have produced its antithesis if the increment in persons convicted . . . was drawn from those who would not have been convicted if they had chanced trial or who would have been dismissed had they not pleaded guilty before making motions that would have resulted in dismissal. Thus the prosecutor may be able partially to neutralize *Escobedo* and *Miranda* by offering yet more radical charge and sentence reductions.[10]

Finally, and perhaps most troublesomely in terms of neat theoretical development, is the fact that the criminal justice process is marked at every stage by a high degree of discretion. Thus, the model presented above must be completed by inserting feedback loops which emphasize (1) the discretion inherent in the performance of each of the linkage functions and (2) the discretion found empirically to exist (and documented below) in the implementation of court decisions prescribing behavior for participants in the other agencies. Let us begin by looking at the interrelationships among bail, preventive detention, and plea bargaining as police-court linkages.

The only stated legal purpose and the sole theoretical purpose of bail in America is to assure the untried defendant's appearance at future proceedings. Thus, appellate courts have held that the likelihood of his appearance (as determined by such community ties as family, employment, and property ownership), and not the severity of the offense with which he is charged, should determine the amount of bail. In practice, however, the amount of bail is usually determined by the seriousness of the offense with the result that many defendants (some studies indicate as many as 50 percent of those charged with felonies) must await trial in jail.[11] The objectionable aspect of bail is obviously that persons are being punished before being found guilty (some studies indicating that as many as 16 percent of defendants spending time in jail as a result of the failure to make bail are eventually found innocent).[12] But, if we reform the bail system so as to guarantee the defendant's appearance without perforce imprisoning the indigent, we are immediately confronted with a major policy problem: the establishment of a pretrial device to keep dangerous defendants (who plausibly would commit crimes while awaiting trial) off the streets. Without bail reform, they are detained while awaiting trial along with many other defendants who are not dangerous. With bail reform they are free. Suddenly we realize what the police and the prosecutors have known all along, that the bail system has been performing the major function of preventive detention.

Pretrial custody thus becomes a major issue in the police-court linkage. As the President's Commission on Law Enforcement and the Administration of Justice has pointed out: "The present invisibility of the issue of dangerousness, by preventing judicial review of specific cases, undoubtedly impedes the development of standards and data concerning dangerousness."[13] Thus, as John Kaplan concludes, "much can be said for bringing the existing practices regarding pretrial detention out into the open where they can be evaluated on their own merits, and where they can be effectively regulated."[14] There are, of course, many reasons for opposing a preventive detention policy. Among them, and having the largest effect on the police-courts linkage, is the probability that "a preventive detention system with the necessary accompaniment of investigations and hearings and representation of counsel and appeals necessary to satisfy due process will significantly add to the burden of an already overloaded criminal justice system."[15]

Plea bargaining is another important police-court linkage. The prosecutor plays the key role in plea bargaining. Although a policeman may be removed from office for not making an arrest, a prosecutor cannot ordinarily be removed for a failure to prosecute,[16] and studies indicate that he generally escapes any political consequences for plea bargaining (whereas he might suffer politically for losing a trial).[17] There are times, of course, when he simply cannot prosecute, either because of the unavailability of witnesses or lack of evidence. Most often, however, he will accept a plea of guilty to a lesser charge in exchange for a lighter sentence, either in order to reduce the workload of the courts to focus on the more significant cases or in order to insure a more politically rewarding high percentage of convictions when he does decide to prosecute. As noted above, recent court decisions expanding due process appear to have had the impact of increasing the frequency of plea bargaining, that is, prosecutors try harder to obtain guilty pleas because they are finding lower rates of guilty verdicts by judges.[18] Plausibly, there are additional tensions among police, prosecution, and court officials in determining arrest and charge standards, and hence discretionary efforts by each to maximize his preferences, but the dynamics of such interplay have yet to be subjected to careful inquiry.

Let us now consider the principal court-corrections linkages. Formally, the sentencing function is performed by the courts—the courts are to determine what happens to a defendant who is guilty of some type of criminal misconduct. However, the judiciary's approach to sentencing as a linkage function is dependent upon variables sometimes beyond its control and upon influences generated by officials in other agencies. Some examples follow. Until quite recently, legislatures tended to grant courts great discretion in sentencing, which at least some judges would have preferred to do without, desiring instead more certainty and predictability in sentencing standards (thus reducing the agony of the decision). On the other hand, recent legislative attempts to enact mandatory sentencing requirements may deny to judges the needed discretion to be at least occasionally flexible in sentencing. Either way, the judiciary is guided, in part, by legislative action. Further, prosecutors are increasingly boxing in overworked judges with guilty pleas won through bargaining. The empirical evidence indicates that although judges may sometimes dominate and so control pretrial bargaining as to produce results they desire, the more common result (and increasingly so) is that they must acquiesce in "agreements" presented to them. It has been hypothesized that plea bargaining is structured, to begin with, by pressures applied through police officials, but to date, most studies of police behavior (as either dependent or independent variable) have concentrated on police-community relations rather than on police-prosecutor or police-court relations. These latter two relationships are perhaps more in need of investigation than any other issues mentioned in this chapter.

Corrections agencies have done very little to consciously influence sentencing practices. As noted below, corrections officials have little opportunity to interact with courts procedurally. This may be unfortunate for at least two reasons. First, the courts, in expanding due process requirements, have seriously limited their own sentencing alternatives, and need input from corrections officials. Second, empirical findings of such potential applicability as the observation that "no matter how likely a type of offender is to repeat criminal activity, he will do better if, instead of being released at the expiration of his sentence, the transition between prison and freedom is made less abrupt by a period of parole,"[19] are rarely if ever exchanged between agencies. These latter points help to emphasize that, at least hypothetically, not all interaction among agencies need be fragmenting.

Judicial Impact and Correctional Isolation. Perhaps one of the most fragmenting features which have been observed in the criminal justice system is the general inability of courts to secure compliance with their decisions by law appliers let alone supportive attitude changes. Let us take as example the Supreme Court decision in *Miranda v. Arizona*[20] which held that criminal suspects must be advised, before interrogation, of their right to remain silent, that anything they say could be used against them, of their right to counsel, and of their right to free, appointed counsel if they cannot afford to pay their own. One study which examined the impact of *Miranda* in law appliers (in this case, police) during a three month period following the decision, found that only 25 of 118 suspects questioned in the jurisdiction covered by the study had been advised of all their rights by police (as spelled out in *Miranda*).[21] On the other hand, only 26 of the 118 suspects received none of the advice required. The right to remain silent was given most frequently—to 90 of the suspects. Eighty-one were told that they had the right to counsel, 51 were told that anything they might say could be held against them, and 27 were advised of their right to appointed counsel.[22] While the rate of compliance with *Miranda* did increase toward the end of the three month period, that compliance was by and large only with the letter and not the spirit of the law. Most of the police

incorporated into their tactical repertoire some sort of hedging on the warnings, when they were given. Some changed the warning slightly: "Whatever you say may be used for or against you in a court of law." Often, the detective advised the suspect with some inconsistent qualifying remark, such as "you don't have to say a word, but you ought to get everything cleared up."[23]

Another study also concerned with the impact of *Miranda* but principally with the impact on the law recipients, the suspects themselves, found that although most suspects had a cognitive understanding of their rights, they had no appreciation of them nor any ability to apply them.[24] For example, more than one-third of those defendants who were advised of their right to counsel nevertheless failed to request it. And 40 percent of those advised of their right to remain silent gave statements to the police despite the warning. When advice was not given, defendants were strikingly more negligent in demanding their rights, indicating perhaps a lack of awareness of the *Miranda* requirements. When no advice was given, fully 75 percent failed to request counsel and more than half gave statements to the police.[25]

Further, some studies have indicated a change in attitude inconsistent with the policy goals of the judicial decision. For example, in examining the impact of the Supreme Court's 1961 decision excluding illegally obtained evidence from state court proceedings,[26] Stuart Nagel found changes of various kinds in the attitudes of law appliers and recipients. Although this so-called exclusionary rule had been in effect in federal courts for a number of years prior to 1961, only about half the states had adopted it by that time. This enabled Nagel to add to his consideration the question as to whether there were any differences in attitude change between people in previously exclusionary and previously nonexclusionary states. If one of the attitudinal objectives of the exclusionary rule is to increase the public's feeling of security from illegal police searches, it was only barely achieved. In fact, 73 percent of Nagel's respondents indicated they saw no change of attitude on this matter in their community, although there was a greater tendency to notice the intended change of attitude on the part of respondents from states which previously had no exclusionary rule. Examining the attitude changes of his total sample of police chiefs, prosecutors, judges, defense attorneys, and ACLU officials, Nagel found two changes in the intended direction: (1) a greater tendency to agree that federal and state police should be under the same rules, and (2) a greater tendency to disagree with the argument that reliable evidence should be admitted regardless of how it was obtained. However, he also found three changes in attitude in the aftermath of the decision which were clearly not intended or supportive: (1) a greater tendency to believe that what constitutes a reasonable search should be broadened, (2) a greater tendency to believe that there is a need for more flexible search warrants, and (3) a greater tendency to believe that too much emphasis is being given to individual liberty and not enough to public safety. Again, all five of these apparent shifts in attitude occurred particularly in states which before 1961 had no exclusionary rule.[27]

Stephen Wasby has attempted to explain this general lack of compliance as follows:

It has been suggested that there is a considerable difference between what Herbert Packer calls the Due Process Model of law enforcement, involving an adversary approach, and utilized by the courts in considering most criminal procedure questions, and the Crime Control Model, in which managerial considerations of law enforcement and order maintenance are paramount. Lack of congruence between the two models, or between the views of . . . judges and law enforcement personnel, helps explain lack of impact of court decisions in this area. So does the general organization of police departments, which are often quite decentralized and the fact that, of everyone on the force, the policeman on the beat had the greatest individual discretion to act. To obtain due process of law, Wilson writes, "requires administrative regularity, strongly enforced department rules, and central authority. These are weakened, and thus regard for the rule of law is weakened, by centralization." Where a police department is most concerned about order maintenance (rather than law enforcement), "central command (is necessary) to insure a reasonably common definition of appropriate order . . . and the protection of the civil liberties of suspects and witnesses."[28]

Finally, some mention must be made of the isolation of corrections agencies, as that isolation affects the feedback system bringing offenders back before the police and the courts. John Kaplan's comments are directly relevant here. The corrections agencies are: (1) physically isolated from the institutions in which offenders are tried and from the communities in which they live (and must survive in if they are to remain outside the system upon release); (2) procedurally isolated from the officials of other agencies (police and courts) in the system, correctional officials having little if any working relationships with them (except for occasional academic workshops); (3) formally isolated from the legal process since the prison's internal operations are rarely scrutinized by appellate courts; and (4) fiscally isolated in that although rehabilitation is its theoretical goal and two-thirds of all persons being "corrected" are on probation or parole, four-fifths of all correctional money is expended on prisons and nine-tenths of all correctional employees work in prisons.[29] There should be little surprise, then, that such a high percentage of the two-thirds temporarily on the outside find themselves, sooner or later, working their way back through the police-court-corrections complex.

The Interagency Exchange System. We will end this chapter with a summary of Cole's conclusions on interagency exchange relationships utilizing the prosecutor's office as the focal organization. First, there is the generalization that most decisions result from some variety of exchange behavior. The prosecutor is likely to play boundary-spanning games more frequently with the courts, community leaders, and county commissioners while the deputy prosecutors interact more frequently with the police and defense attorneys. Second, although the prosecutor is limited in his discretion by the willingness of the police to provide inputs in the form of cases and evidence (he is limited because he has scarce investigative resources of his own), he has superior countervailing power in his authority to disapprove arrest warrants and to return cases to the police for further investigation. Sometimes the prosecutor will return cases to the police for no reason other than his desire to check the quality of police work. Further, by cultivating cordial relations with the press, the prosecutor can shift the blame for crime to the police, and by refusing their input he can damage their discipline and morale, at least if his refusal to accept cases is sustained over time. Third, the courts structure the decision to prosecute in that a judge's sentencing history serves as an indicator of how easily a prosecutor can expect to control the flow of cases through plea bargaining. The courts' decisions respecting plea bargaining in turn affect the pressures on the correctional agencies and the workload of probation officers. But fourth, and last, the courts themselves are constrained by pressures brought to bear by the correctional agencies. Cole quotes one county judge as stating: "When the number of prisoners gets to the 'riot point,' the warden puts pressure on us to slow down the flow. This often means that men are let out on parole and the number of people given probation and suspended sentences increases." Obviously, if the judge responds favorably to such pressures, other parts of the exchange system will adjust accordingly.[30]

What are the prescriptions?

In short, the policy scientist must work with the program planner and practitioner to develop rational law enforcement guidelines for the police, charge guidelines for the prosecutors, sentencing guidelines for the courts, and parole guidelines for the parole boards,[31] and to so integrate their functions that the horizontal linkages in criminal justice policy might be more easily described as bridges than as culverts.

7

CIVIL JUSTICE POLICY

As we switch our focus from criminal justice to civil justice, a couple of conventional distinctions should be made between criminal law and ciivl law and, more broadly, between public law and private law. Criminal law governs the behavior of persons by prohibiting acts against society and thus, as we have seen, a criminal action is one in which the state prosecutes a defendant and the outcome is either acquittal or conviction. The court's order in a criminal action in which the defendant is convicted is either a fine or imprisonment or both. Civil law governs the relations between persons (including the state and private persons) involving either a breach of an agreement or a breach of a duty imposed by law (typically actions in torts, contracts, property, and domestic relations). A civil action is one in which the court attempts to determine the legal rights of the parties involved and the outcome is either an award of money damages to the injured party or a court order directing one of the parties to do or to refrain from doing a specified act. Criminal and civil law are thus by definition distinct and the procedural rules governing criminal and civil actions are similarly separate. However, the distinctions should not be pressed too hard. The American legal system does recognize that societal interests may be implicated in purely private civil actions. For instance, in some civil actions the courts will award not merely "compensatory damages" (for example, reimbursements for medical expenses incurred as the result of injury) but also "punitive damages" to punish the wrongdoer for an act that is considered a violation of community norms. Such punitive damages are particularly common in libel and antitrust cases. Moreover, not all civil actions are purely private. The government may be (and quite commonly is) a party to a civil action. On the national level alone, as we have seen, the government is either party plaintiff or party defendant in about thirty percent of the 100,000 civil cases initiated in the U.S. district courts in an average year. These are not criminal cases in which the U.S. attorney is prosecuting an alleged violation of a federal criminal law but civil cases in which the national government is involved, typically, in some sort of tax or contract dispute. The point is that some civil actions do have a public character which brings us to the distinction between public law and private law. Public law is conventionally defined as involving cases in which the state is (though it may not be a party to the suit) either the subject of a legal right or the object of a legal duty and as such includes constitutional law, statutory law, administrative law, and criminal law. Private law is conventionally defined as involving cases in which the state is not implicated either as a party or as a source of a legal obligation. The state merely provides the forum (the court) for the resolution of purely private disputes. According to this definition the realm of private law is limited to those civil actions in which the state is not a party. The functions of public law are said to be the maintenance of law and order, the protection of personal freedoms, and the surveillance of official action, while the functions of private law are said to be the recognition of ownership, the provision for redress of harm and broken agreements, and the reinforcement of the family.[1] Until quite recently, social science research on law has emphasized public law largely to the exclusion of private law and, more specifically, criminal law largely to the exclusion of civil law. There are a number of very good reasons why this ought not to be (and increasingly is not) the case.

First, neither the public law–private law distinction nor the criminal law–civil law distinction seem warranted in light of anthropological and historical evidence. Anthropologically, as we observed in chapter 2, the only meaningful distinction in primitive societies is between law and no law. Primitive persons make no distinction between public and private offenses and to assume that the resolution of a dispute affects no interests other than those of the disputants would simply be false.[2] Historically, in the Anglo-American common law tradition, feudal law constituted the very antithesis of the public law–private law distinction. Under feudal law, for example, tenure conveyed both private property and public office and the ancient action of trespass included some elements which today we conventionally label private and others we label criminal and hence public. Indeed the entire medieval law of torts (including trespass) inextricably intertwined criminal and civil procedures.[3] Second, it would be difficult if possible at all to find any kind of law that does not authoritatively allocate values, and since it is now widely accepted that the task of political science is to study the authoritative allocation of values, it is nearly impossible to make the case that political scientists should study some kinds of law but not others. Third, even today in countries like the United States where the public law–private law distinction is most obviously alive, both types of legal action can arise from the same, single act. For example, if A takes B's watch, that act is both the tort of conversion (to be pursued in a private, civil action) and the crime of larceny (to be prosecuted in a public, criminal action). Similarly, if A intentionally injures B, that act can be dealt with in both civil and criminal litigation. The formal distinctions between private and public, civil and criminal are maintained, but the legal system which allocates justice in both types of actions blithely mixes elements of both.[4] And, just as in primitive societies, the resolution of disputes in purely private civil actions does affect societal interests far beyond the immediate interests of the disputants. For example, a suit by a private person or group of persons against a manufacturer in nuisance or trespass, seeking a court order banning continued operation which pollutes the water or air, is both private and civil. Yet the problem being solved and the interests being protected are clearly public. Indeed, many of the recent attempts to use the legal system to solve policy problems come in the form of private, civil actions. In chapter 8 we will be looking at some of these attempts. In this chapter we will examine the flow of cases in the civil justice process and show that the study of civil justice is entirely consistent with the contemporary policy focus of social science research.

THE DISPUTE AND THE FORUM

A civil dispute reaches a court when the lawyer for a person who thinks he has been wronged files a formal complaint with the clerk of the court specifying the plaintiff's factual contentions constituting a cause of action. But the civil justice process actually commences long before a complaint is filed. Indeed, the dispute may be settled before any court becomes involved. The initial phase of the civil justice process is the exploration conference. Typically, a person who thinks he has been wronged will contact a lawyer and describe his problem. Before the lawyer accepts a retainer, he usually outlines, in general terms, the various alternatives open to the person and requests an opportunity to investigate the matter personally to make an initial determination of whether a legal cause of action exists. This is usually followed by a second meeting at which the lawyer spells out the likelihood of winning the case in court, the exact remedies available, and the amount of damages the plaintiff can expect to receive if he wins the case. If the plaintiff still wants to proceed, he retains the lawyer who then notifies the defendant that his client intends to seek an adjudicative settlement against him. The defendant is then likely to retain a lawyer almost immediately and the first out-of-court settlement conference phase ensues.[5] Here, the opposing lawyers meet, with or without their clients, to negotiate a reasonable settlement. Settlement conferences are somewhat analogous to the plea-bargaining phase of the criminal justice process. If counsel for the plaintiff can save himself the time and money that goes into preparing a case for trial by accepting from the defendant a sum of money just slightly less than what he would ask for in court, he usually will do so. Since he has probably been retained on what is called a "contingency fee" (according to which he receives a percentage of the award if he wins in court but nothing if he loses), plaintiff's counsel is induced to accept a negotiated settlement. In fact, some studies show that as many as forty percent of all civil disputes are settled at this stage without any kind of court action having taken place. If, however, these negotiations fail to produce a settlement, the plaintiff's lawyer prepares to go to court. His first decision is the selection of a forum.

In most civil cases the plaintiff's lawyer has a choice between several state trial courts where there is overlapping jurisdiction, and in "diversity cases" (cases in which the two parties are citizens of different states and the sum of money in controversy exceeds $10,000) he has a choice between state courts and the U.S. district court. His strategy in "forum shopping" is to choose that court which will most likely respond favorably to his objectives. Although there is little empirical evidence on the matter, it is now conventional to assume that the factors most commonly associated with the choice of forum are the quality and known biases of the judges, the benefits of differing rules of procedure, and geographic convenience.[6] There is little evidence, however, that federal judges are superior or otherwise more professionally qualified than state judges and one study has shown that among the reasons lawyers prefer taking cases to national courts when possible, the quality of the judge ranks only fourth in importance. Of greater importance, apparently, are greater geographic convenience, broader discovery rules, and larger damages awarded by federal juries.[7]

THE PROCESS OF SETTLING CIVIL DISPUTES

After he has selected the forum, the plaintiff's lawyer prepares the summons and complaint. The summons (or "process" as legal jargon would have it) names the party bringing the suit, identifies his lawyer, and identifies the court to which the case will be taken. The complaint formally informs both the defendant and the court of the plaintiff's factual contentions constituting the cause of action. It also attempts to establish the court's jurisdiction over the dispute and makes a formal demand for relief. The summons and complaint are served to the defendant either by the sheriff or by a process server and the complaint is also filed with the clerk of the court. The summons warns the defendant that unless he responds within a stated time a default judgment may be entered against him for the relief which the plaintiff has demanded. Once the complaint has been filed the initiative shifts to the defendant's lawyer who has a number of options open to him. He may respond by filing a demurrer, or motion to dismiss. The demurrer contends that even if the facts as alleged by the plaintiff are true there is no legal cause of action and no legal basis for granting relief. If the judge agrees and sustains the demurrer, the plaintiff will either seek to amend his complaint or simply drop the case. If the judge overrules the demurrer the defendant's lawyer must prepare his answer to the complaint. The answer may admit that some of the facts alleged in the complaint are true and these "stipulated" facts need not be discussed or proved at the trial. The answer will also contain denials. The facts that are denied and which, if not true, would prevent the plaintiff from prevailing constitute the defense. The allegations (in the complaint) and the denials (in the answer) structure the factual issues to be proved in court. The answer may also include a counterclaim alleging wrong doing by the plaintiff and seeking relief against him. The plaintiff may also file a reply to the defendant's answer. The complaint, answer, and reply constitute the "pleadings" in the case and once all pleadings have been filed the issue is said to be "joined."

At this juncture, a number of pretrial motions may be made. Either party may move for a "summary judgment" which is intended to dispose of disputes in which the material facts cannot be proved. If the moving party can provide documentary proof illustrating that the other party's factual allegations cannot be proved or are false the motion is granted. Also, a pretrial motion for "judgment on the pleadings" may be made not questioning the facts in the pleadings but the legal sufficiency of the pleadings. Like the demurrer, motions for a judgment on the pleadings raise only questions of law not fact. Neither summary judgments nor judgments on the pleadings will be granted if there is a real issue of fact between the parties because this would deny to the losing party his right to a trial.[8] Prior to trial, the lawyers may also make motions requesting the judge to permit interrogation of the other party or his witnesses. These interrogations take various forms and are referred to collectively as "discovery." Discovery is based on the premise that each party is ultimately entitled to a judgment based on all the information available including the known facts, the location of witnesses, the opinions of experts, and the existence of documents. The two most common tools of discovery are depositions and interrogatories. Depositions may be oral or written and are answered by witnesses. If the deposition is oral, it occurs before a court official with the opposing party present to cross-examine the witness. Interrogatories are similar to written depositions in that both are lists of written questions to be answered in writing under oath but interrogatories can be administered only to the parties, not to witnesses.[9] Pretrial motions and discovery are not the only activities or even the most significant activities which occur during the three- to six-month period of delay which commonly intervenes between the filing of pleadings and the trial. A second series of out-of-court settlement conferences resembling plea bargaining usually takes place during this time. For the reasons mentioned above, both sides are induced to settle out of court. Also by this time other informal participants such as insurance adjustors and real estate brokers have become involved in the case and they too see an advantage in rapid disposition of the conflict. In fact, about thirty-three percent of all civil disputes are settled at this stage.

Should these negotiations fail, there is one last attempt at settlement at the pretrial conference. In theory, the pretrial conference between the judge and the two lawyers is designed to simplify the case so that it will take up as little of the court's precious time as possible. The judge attempts to persuade the lawyers to agree on certain facts so that these undisputed or stipulated facts may be merely entered in the record and not contested in court. He may also seek to clear away the underbrush by persuading the lawyers to remove from their pleadings issues which they do not really intend to raise in court but which they have packed into their pleadings either to impress their clients or to insure themselves against surprises.[10] In recent years, however, judges have also used the pretrial conference to encourage negotiation and to induce a pretrial settlement, even to the point of suggesting a particular sum of money the two sides might reasonably settle upon.[11] About sixteen percent of all civil disputes are settled at the pretrial conference. That leaves only about eleven percent of all civil cases which actually go to trial.

Because of the frequent contact between the opposing lawyers during the negotiation and discovery phases of the civil justice process, the few cases which do go to trial rarely produce dramatic surprises, Perry Mason's

FIGURE 5. THE CIVIL JUSTICE PROCESS

1. *Exploration Conference*
2. *First Series of Out-of-Court Settlement Conferences.* (About 40 percent of all civil disputes are settled at this stage).
3. *Forum Shopping and Selection.*

4. *Filing Pleadings.* (Summons and complaint, answer and possible counterclaim, reply)
5. *Pretrial Motions and Discovery*
6. *Second Series of Out-of-Court Settlement Conferences.* (About 33 percent of all civil disputes are settled at this stage.

7. *Pretrial Conference.* (About 16 percent of all civil disputes are settled at this stage.)
8. *Trial.* (About 11 percent of all civil disputes go to trial.)

courtroom antics to the contrary notwithstanding. The trial procedure is fairly routine. The plaintiff's lawyer presents his case and the defendant's lawyer presents his case. The plaintiff's lawyer may then present witnesses or exhibits to rebut the case of the defense. Each side then makes a summation. At this point either side may make a motion for a directed verdict which the judge will grant only if he is convinced that reasonable persons could not possibly disagree on the outcome. If there is a jury and there has been no directed verdict, the judge then summarizes the case and gives a charge to the jury in which he explains what facts they need to find in order to reach a particular verdict. The jury's verdict is not necessarily final however. The losing party may move for a judgment "n.o.v." (notwithstanding the verdict), which the judge will grant only if he is convinced that reasonable persons could not possibly reach the verdict that the jury reached.

CIVIL CASE DECISIONS AS POLICY

As we observed above in this chapter, the civil justice process is no less involved in authoritatively allocating values in America than is the criminal justice process though its impact is less direct and less frequently acknowledged. Civil cases in which the government is a party do get some attention. Governments are plaintiffs in suits to acquire needed land, in actions seeking compliance by private companies with contracts entered into with government agencies, and, on the national level, in antitrust suits. Governments are defendants in taxpayer suits, in prisoner's rights cases, in welfare and environmental actions, in suits arising from injuries sustained on government property, and in cases challenging the implementation of government programs (for example, Medicaid).[12] But even when the government is not a party to a civil action, the case can have a policy impact. Although a relatively small percentage of civil cases involve public policy directly, many affect societal interests much broader than those of the two litigants. For example, civil suits for debt commonly result in garnishment, liens, and forced sale of the debtor's property in cases in which plaintiffs win by default (because the defendant fails to appear) and in which incompetent judges grant default judgments even though legal service of the summons was clearly improper.[13] Clearly, not only do such decisions affect the allocation of wealth in society but also formal governmental power sustains the action. Cases are decided by courts, merchandise is repossessed by police, and auctions of seized property are conducted by sheriffs.[14]

There are, of course, other types of civil cases which involve public policy much more directly. Courts in civil cases pass upon legislative districting schemes, interpret voter registration requirements, determine the validity of nominating petitions and the excessiveness of candidate filing fees, and decide cases involving attempts by independent candidates to appear on election ballots. They also decide such cases as those involving the power of annexation, the regulation of business, and the power to tax. Thus, civil courts deal directly with questions concerning who serves in positions of power and, by interpreting the rules of the game, determine what powers can be exercised. They can also influence the specific content of public policy itself in such cases as those involving zoning, land use, civil rights, and labor relations.[15] And it must be remembered that these cases are rarely settled out of court. They usually go to trial because the plaintiff is more concerned with policy results than with the protection of his personal interests and the pursuit of policy normally requires litigation that passes on to some form of final appellate review which would be unavailable if the dispute were settled out of court.[16]

Clearly, civil cases can be an important part of the policy process. Most of the cases we will refer to in the next chapter (in which we attempt to analyze the use of courts to solve policy problems) are civil cases.

PART THREE

LAW AND PUBLIC POLICY: TOWARD A JURIDICAL POLICY SCIENCE

The purpose of part 3 is to analyze the legal process as a tool for solving policy problems and to determine whether the social scientific study of questions left unanswered by jurisprudence has as yet produced a "juriscience."

8

ADJUDICATION OF POLICY ISSUES

INTRODUCTION

As we have seen, law is a political phenomenon. Law consists of rules subject to enforcement by politically organized government, and politics consists of the process by which public policy is formulated and executed. Thus is produced an ancient and inescapable interrelationship: law determines the scope of politics, and politics determines the content of law. The data of politics includes "the behaviors of participants in the government, whether or not such activities fit the specifications of the legal blueprints."[1] Thus, some of the participants in the legal system are official—litigants, lawyers, judges, and juries—and others are unofficial— interest groups and the media. But materials bearing upon the roles of all of these participants in the legal system in formulating public policy provide one kind of political data.[2]

It is not necessary in this chapter either to enter or to resolve the pro- longed debate among social scientists as to whether judges consciously "make" law or mechanically "interpret" it. We do know, as Plato sug- gested, that perfectly simple principles cannot be applied to a state of affairs which is the reverse of simple. Or, as put more recently by Justice Holmes, general propositions do not decide concrete cases. The implica- tion is, obviously, that if rules of law do not in themselves decide disputes, judges must. Whether they are defining the Constitution, or construing statutes, or applying analogies in case law, judges must necessarily choose between alternative and often competing interpretations, and in doing so they exercise discretion. Perhaps they recognize this leeway for discretion and act accordingly to optimize their personal policy objectives. Perhaps they do not. For our purposes in this chapter it does not really matter because regardless of their motivations, their output is a political product. Judges are in the political process and their activity is interest activity, not necessarily as a matter of choice, but always as a matter of function.[3]

In short, law is a political instrument.[4] Legal order is a vital part of political order, and the legal process both defines and is defined by the political process. The legal system, as we have defined it, includes legislative and administrative institutions and processes as well as judicial ones. But we are concentrating here on the judiciary, and examining just one of its many political aspects. Precisely, our objective is to answer the question: What potential is there in the legal system for resolving political problems?

We will note that techniques have been devised to enhance accessibility to the legal system by participants not directly involved in a particular case or controversy and to broaden the scope of political conflict within the judicial arena generally. This is important because problem solvers cannot ordinarily advance their interests in the judicial arena in the same manner as they can in the legislative arena. For example, our norms prohibit direct contact with judges (button-holing judges in the traditional "lobbying" sense). However, interest groups have found alternative mechanisms. The four most common means of access to the judiciary utilized by interest groups are (1) passing information along to judges by writing articles for legal periodicals, (2) submitting amicus curiae (friend of the court) briefs, (3) instituting test cases, and (4) organizing class actions.

We do have some evidence that judges read and are influenced by law review articles. Some observers have argued that liberal judges read and are influenced by law review articles more frequently than conservative ones. If this is true, it may be explained by the fact that conservatives are less likely to find support for their views there. In any event, none of this evidence is very solid, and the impact of law review articles on judicial decision making remains extremely difficult to measure.

Submitting amicus curiae briefs is a much more direct means of influencing judicial decisions. These briefs are technically intended to give to the court information and arguments not otherwise presented and thus provide a broader basis for decision. They may simply complement the

brief of a litigant or they may advise the court of the probable consequences of an adverse decision. In practice, of course, they enable interested parties to place their opinions and attitudes on the record, and in the
sense that they rely principally upon the utility of information they
parallel most strikingly the technique of lobbying before legislatures.[5] In
recent years the use of amicus curiae briefs has increased rapidly, with 107
briefs submitted to the United States Supreme Court in 1961 alone.[6]
There are, however, certain restrictions and costs. To file a brief, an
interested party must first receive permission from the litigants or the
court. Even if permission is granted, amicus curiae briefs may evoke
similar briefs from the adversary. And there is little evidence that judges
are influenced by them.[7] Nevertheless, interest groups do perceive the
amicus curiae brief as a useful means of influencing judicial policy making.
In the recent case of *De Funis v. Odegaard*[8] involving a preferential law
school admissions policy, for example, amicus curiae briefs were submitted
by virtually every civil rights group, by fifty-nine law schools, by the
AFL–CIO, and by the UAW. Big legal names also wrote amicus curiae
briefs in *De Funis.* Alexander Bickel and Philip Kurland collaborated on
a brief for the Anti-Defamation League opposing special preferences while
Archibald Cox and former Solicitor General Erwin Griswold supported
the policy in a brief for the American Association of Law Schools. At
minimum, the opportunity to submit amicus curiae briefs provides interested groups with access to the judiciary.

The test case is an even more direct means of obtaining favorable
judicial action. Ordinarily, the tactic is to intentionally violate a law in
order to have "standing" in the courts and thus provide judges with an
opportunity to interpret the law or the Constitution in a manner consistent with the group's goals. The test case has been used successfully
in winning important policy changes, most notably by such groups as the
N.A.A.C.P. and the Jehovah's Witnesses. Again, there are some obstacles
to utilizing the test case effectively. A group cannot institute a test case
unless it first finds someone who is willing to violate the law. Even if such
a person is found, he may soon tire of the case and back out, or more
commonly, he may lose standing before the case reaches the court. This
has been a problem in the area of school integration where the student
is out of school before the case is concluded and therefore no longer an
aggrieved party. Finally, even if a litigant is found and he does maintain
standing, the court may decide the case against him, or, for him, but on
grounds other than those anticipated to solve the problem.

Some of these difficulties, particularly the standing problem,[9] have been overcome by the use of class actions. In some instances a litigant can file a case not only for himself but also for all others "similarly situated." This can be an important technique for at least two reasons. First, if one litigant should lose standing, a substitute can replace him. Second, if the court decides the case consistently with the policy goals of the instigator, that decision will be assured a much broader application. (As we shall see, the class action has been particularly useful in the area of consumer protection.) To obtain a class action, the petition must allege that the class in question is so numerous that joinder of all members is impractical, that there are questions of fact or law common to all members of the class, that the claims made are typical for the class represented, and that the plaintiffs will raise all arguments and defenses necessary to protect the interest of the class.[10] Obviously, a successfully executed class action provides a much broader remedy than is otherwise obtainable. However, in the recent case of *Eisen v. Carlisle & Jacquelin*,[11] the Supreme Court "cast a shadow on the feasibility of class actions ... as a tool for accomplishing social change"[12] by holding that when class action suits are brought on behalf of very large numbers of people (in this case two million) those bringing the suit must notify individually each member of the class who is readily identifiable and pay for the cost of the notice as part of the ordinary burden of financing the suit. In the past, notification had been made inexpensively by newspaper announcements. Now, however, the burdens and costs of identifying and notifying all the members of the class will probably preclude many class action suits.

LAW AS BOTH EFFECT AND CAUSE

In our examination of the potential in the courts for solving political problems, we will consider law as both effect and cause. In other words, we are going to consider law as both the response of lawmakers to prior stimuli and as stimuli to the subsequent responses of law appliers and law recipients.[13] If an actor (individual or group) wishes to utilize the legal system as a tool for solving a particular problem, he must first obtain a favorable decision from the lawmakers. But the process does not stop with this favorable "output." In order to solve the problem, the actor must see to it that the decision is implemented by the law appliers and adhered to by the law recipients in such a way as to at least minimally satisfy his goals. This final result in society, the "outcome," is the only true test of his success but it is also usually more difficult to achieve than the simple court decision and decree.

First, we will consider the problems of influencing lawmakers prior to implementation. Second, we will examine the problems of impact and compliance. Our thesis is that (1) law may not be the only means but it is clearly the most significant means of implementing social policy, and (2) the courts possess a potential, though not an unlimited one, to solve political problems.

LAW AS RESPONSE TO PRIOR STIMULI

The proponent of reform who wishes to work within the framework of the judicial process to achieve his goals might be easily encouraged to believe that he can successfully stimulate judicial policy makers to render decisions favorable to his cause. In recent years the development of case law in the United States has played a significant role in bringing about social reform. The courts have condemned separate public educational facilities for children of different races,[14] required political representation to be based on population,[15] and held that the destitute not be deprived of such fundamental rights as a fair trial and appellate review.[16] More recently, reformers have begun to use the legal system to solve problems in the areas of environmental defense, consumer protection, and welfare rights. Let us examine some of the legal tools for problem solving in these last three issue areas.

Environmental Defense. Although environmental defense was of little general interest before the mid 1960s, the ranks of environmentalists concerned with the increasing destruction of man's natural resources have steadily swelled in recent years. They have often turned to the courts for help, and usually they have received it. This is not to say that legislative bodies have been unresponsive to their demands. Congress, in its National Environmental Policy Act of 1969, established a long-range goal of restoring "environmental quality," required the President to submit an annual Environmental Quality Report to Congress, and created a Council on Environmental Quality to evaluate existing programs and recommend improvements. Congress has also passed various air and water pollution laws and refuse disposal regulations, and has created the Environmental

Protection Agency to deal with a wide variety of potential dangers to the environment. State and local legislative bodies have been even more sensitive to environmental problems.[17] However, as is often the case with reformist legislation, the problem has been one of enforcement and of accommodation with competing considerations, in this case business interests and economic growth. Rigid enforcement of environmental laws can cause not only the loss of thousands of dollars for business but also the loss of thousands of jobs for the community. Thus, the primary role of courts in this issue area has been to accommodate between environmental and economic interests.

When there is no legislation which the environmentalist can use, his principal legal tool is the common law concept of nuisance, as we observed in chapter 5. For example, as pointed out in chapter 5, if B's home air conditioner produces an unusually loud noise causing A, an adjoining home owner, great discomfort, a court can compensate A with money damages and enjoin B from further use of his air conditioner. Analogously, if a factory emits a substance into the air which damages A's property, A may be awarded damages and the factory may be enjoined from further such emissions. In each instance, the pollution caused is a nuisance and may be legally banned.[18]

The environmentalist, of course, would like to develop a much broader legal tool, and many think they have found it in the Ninth Amendment which states that individual rights under the Constitution are not limited to those rights specifically enumerated. The Supreme Court has already included in the Ninth Amendment the right to privacy, and environmentalists argue that the individual's right to an environment free from pollution ought to be similarly included.[19] To date, the Supreme Court has not agreed to do so. However, the federal courts have shown considerable sensitivity to the environmental issue. In *U.S. v. Bishop Processing Co.,*[20] for example, the Fourth Circuit Court of Appeals affirmed a district court decree ordering the defendant company, an animal reduction plant, to cease all of its processing and manufacturing operations due to the fetid air pollution caused by its operations. The court said in part:

Pollution is a severe and increasing problem of which the courts and other branches of government have become acutely conscious. The residents of the area in the neighborhood of Bishop's plant have the right to demand that the air they breathe shall not be defiled by what witnesses described as a "horrible" and "nauseating" stench.

. . . .

The court is not unmindful of the serious consequences to appellant's business. . . . [But the remedy] seems inescapable since Bishop has over a long period failed to take effective measures to solve the problem.

It is difficult to predict at this point whether the courts will begin to enlarge the arsenal of legal weapons to combat pollution either by incorporating "environmental rights" into the Bill of Rights or by some other means. However, we do have evidence that courts are increasingly sensitive to the problem and are presently willing to extend existing legal concepts to their limits in order to better provide for environmental defense. Certainly, major interest groups such as the Sierra Club, the National Wildlife Federation, the Friends of the Earth, Zero Population Growth, the Izaak Walton League, and the Environmental Defense Fund (EDF) have been active as litigants and as amicus curiae before the courts, especially the U.S. Supreme Court. Although these groups are somewhat restricted by their economic resources in pressing litigation (especially as compared with industry trade groups whom they commonly oppose such as the Lake Carrier's Association), they do use participating lawyers who volunteer their services and have met with some success. The EDF, for example, employs sixty lawyers, seven hundred scientists, and many other volunteers in an organization of 25,000 members working to present cases in the courts. The EDF has, to date, successfully banned DDT in several states and then nationally, delayed construction of the Alaskan pipeline, and blocked plans for three major canal and dam projects.[21]

Clearly, environmental law is essentially a product of the decade of the 1970s and that means, in terms of court-made policy, that it is largely the work of the Burger Court. In general, the record of the Burger Court has been favorable to environmental interests. The standing to sue doctrine has been broadened and judicial enforcement of NEPA has produced increased administrative disclosures, more detailed analysis of environmental impact, and more careful future planning concerning the environment by federal agencies. There is some indication, however, that since Justice Douglas's departure from the Court, more conservative judicial approaches to environmental defense are growing in influence.[22]

Consumer Protection. The legal system also has provided an increasingly attractive forum for advocates of consumer protection. Again, the problem is not necessarily that legislative bodies have been particularly remiss in their efforts. For example, legislatures have commonly barred from sale various kinds of products which can injure consumers such as unsafe toys and dangerous foods and drugs. (And Congress is currently investigating the potential risk to athletes from playing on artificial turf.) Various antitrust laws prohibit most types of price-fixing agreements and unfair trade practices. The Truth in Lending Act stipulates that lenders must inform borrowers of the true cost of their loan. These and other legislative measures have gone a long way to advance the rights of consumers. But the judicial process affords an additional and alternative forum for action. And, as in the area of environmental defense, courts are showing increasing sensitivity to the complaints of litigants.

Traditionally, the two legal principles which grant protection to consumers are (1) they may sue their immediate seller and those who were involved in the manufacture or distribution of dangerous products if the failure to exercise reasonable care caused injury, and (2) they may sue anyone who specifically promised that the product in question possessed qualities which it did not and the absence of such qualities caused injury.[23] Remedies typically include (1) compensatory damages for bodily injuries, hospital expenses and loss of earnings, (2) relief in the form of refunded money, and (3) in some cases, punitive damages against the wrongdoer which penalize him and deter others from similar conduct. However, courts and administrative agencies have tended in recent years to take three different steps in the direction of affording even greater protection to consumers. First, they have been giving more liberal interpretations to the terms "aggrieved party" and "standing to sue," thus opening up the legal process to more litigants. Second, many states have established small claims courts in which the cost of processing claims is small and procedures are simplified, so that the consumer whose loss is small and who might otherwise therefore find court costs prohibitive, may now seek redress more easily. Third, and perhaps most importantly, courts have increasingly accepted class actions in the area of consumer protection. Consumer litigation is one area in which class suits can be used most effectively because the businessman who might not fear an individual suit for damages, will certainly fear a potential court decision favorable to thousands of consumers. If all consumers injured in a manner similar to the injury to the litigant in a class suit can receive payment under the terms of the court's judgment in that suit, the defendant might have to pay thousands, even millions of dollars in damages. Clearly, such a possibility induces the businessman to be more careful in his relations with consumers.[24] A large toy manufacturer, for example, may not fear a single suit for $25,000 in damages, but the possibility of having to pay $25,000 to each of thousands of litigants is an inducement to the manufacture of safe toys.

Welfare Rights. In the third area of discussion, welfare rights, reformers have not been quite as successful, even though they have an abundance of legal tools at their disposal. The class action, the utilization of neighborhood legal-aid services, and the principle of *in forma pauperis* have all become common characteristics of poverty litigation in the United States. But even though some advances have been made, welfare recipients are frequent losers in court actions even when all of these legal tools are utilized.

The principle of *in forma pauperis* (literally, "to proceed as a poor person") has increasingly assisted indigent parties in protecting or securing their rights in courts. In effect, the principle allows them to avoid the cost of the action and the necessity of providing security. However, *in forma pauperis* itself is not a legal right but a privilege granted in each case at the discretion of the court. If, in a given case, the court decides that it is unlikely that the poor person will win his case, the request to proceed *in forma pauperis* will be turned down. If, on the other hand, it appears that the poor person, with adequate counsel and in a true adversary situation, can probably win his case, the request will be granted. Obviously, *in forma pauperis* does not result in according identical legal rights to the poor and the rich alike. The rich, because of their resources, possess too many natural advantages in the legal process to be overcome by this one principle (for example, they are more likely to obtain talented counsel, competent investigators, expert witnesses, etc.). But *in forma pauperis* has served to ameliorate this situation to some degree.

Legal-aid services, though nothing new, became more accessible tools for the poor as a result of the Economic Opportunity Act of 1964. For many years prior to that, local bar associations commonly sponsored legal-aid societies which, as a charitable service, provided a variety of legal assistance to the poor.[25] OEO legal services built upon that base. OEO legal service programs were ordinarily nonprofit enterprises incorporated under state law, and frequently they used and built upon programs previously created by local bar associations. The OEO financed the programs to 90 percent of their operating budget. The remaining 10 percent came from the community and often took the form of volunteer service or equipment donated by local business. Although ultimately vulnerable to legislative and administrative regulation, the OEO legal services program came a long way in achieving its objective of "providing a limited nature of social change by alleviating some of the shocking conditions of impoverished life by providing a free and valuable service."[26] Legal-aid services, despite the withdrawal of much legislative and administrative support, are much more easily accessible in the 1970s than ever before.

However, even with these various tools at their command, the poor are facing what one commentator has labeled "judicial retrenchment in welfare adjudication."[27] Let us take as an example the challenge made in *Dandridge v. Williams*[28] of maximum grant provisions under the Aid to Families with Dependent Children program. In nearly half of the states there are either administrative regulations or statutory norms which establish a ceiling on the amount payable to a family under the federally funded AFDC. Although these maximum grant provisions take a variety of forms they usually impose an arbitrary dollar ceiling. In *Williams*, for example, the Maryland Department of Social Services had established a $250 per month ceiling regardless of the size of the family to which it was to be paid. The Williams family numbered nine. Interestingly, applying federal poverty standards (that is, the amount required for subsistence as defined by the Social Security Administration) we find that the amount required for a family of seven or more is $433.75 per month. And, even if we apply the regular schedules of the Maryland Department of Public Welfare, we find the amount required to satisfy basic needs is $296.15 per month. Yet, under Maryland's maximum grant provision for families on AFDC, the Williams family received only $250 per month. This tendency of maximum grant provisions to reduce the recipient's level of support below even the level of state-computed need is typical of provisions in 40 percent of the states. Such situations have served to generate an increasing amount of litigation challenging the validity of welfare standards. In this case, the Williams family proceeded *in forma pauperis*, and with the assistance of a neighborhood legal-aid service (specifically, three attorneys from Legal Aid East in Baltimore), to bring a class action against the maximum grant provision. But the Supreme Court, by a 5–3 vote, found the state policy permissible.[29]

Thus, we can see that the response of courts to stimuli provided by various social reformers has been mixed. On balance, however, the courts are more frequently becoming agents of social change. The class action, the use of legal-aid services, the appearance of amicus curiae, and the principle of *in forma pauperis* are just some of the legal tools which the reformer can utilize.

LAW AS STIMULI TO SUBSEQUENT RESPONSES

When the problem solver successfully obtains a judicial decision and decree satisfying his goals, he has won, at most, only half the battle. He is now confronted with a whole new range of obstacles which complicate the implementation process. He must ask himself: What will be the final results in society of this decision?

There is a substantial body of both scholarly and popular belief which might persuade him that very little, if anything, will happen in society. The notion that law cannot induce social change is evident in sociologist William Graham Sumner's assertion that "stateways cannot change folkways." That same contention is apparent in the currently popular slogan, "You can't legislate morality." The central tenet of this line of reasoning, as pointed out by Frederick M. Wirt, is that man's established patterns of behavior are the product of man's preferences, and public policy is therefore the product of dominant values, explicit forms of implicit preferences.[30] Thus, laws reflect what is prevalent but they cannot lead man where he will not go. Cited in support of this thesis are the American experiences with prohibition and laws prohibiting abortion, homosexuality, and drug abuse. In the area of racial equality, the argument is made that court decisions outlawing discrimination cannot work because you cannot counter racial instincts of prejudice.

In opposition to this position there are those who argue that a distinction must be made between attitudes and behavior when assessing a law's impact. In fact, these people argue, it is behavior not attitudes which is the law's target.[31] For example, in utilizing the legal system as an instrument for reform in the area of race relations, it is not the attitude of prejudice which is initially attacked but discriminatory behavior. The objective is to equalize external conditions and lessen discrimination by guaranteeing minority groups equal access to the ballot, equal educational opportunities, increased skills, and a higher standard of living. Such an approach, it is argued, creates a standard of behavior which checks at least overt signs of prejudice.[32] As a final result, these behavioral changes will produce attitude changes as well. In other words, "The masses of people do not become converts in advance; rather they are converted by the fait accompli. . . . They allow themselves to be re-educated by the new norm that prevails."[33] In support of this argument, Wirt cites findings which show that laws bringing races together in conditions of equality produce lowered prejudice as a result of altered perceptions of blacks. Cited as examples are the results of integrated conditions in schools, public housing, and the armed services. In short, legal decisions may not change attitudes and behavior completely, but they will act as a restraint. "They will deter whoever is deterrable. They will not deter the compulsive bigot or demagogue. But neither do laws against arson deter the pyromaniac. Laws, we may say, restrain the middle range of mortals who need them as a mentor in molding their habits."[34]

In searching the literature of political science, however, we can find only conflicting evidence as to whether legal decisions alter even the behavior let alone the attitudes of law appliers and recipients. As we observed in chapter 6 when looking at the impact of certain criminal justice decisions, the evidence indicates that law appliers frequently comply with the letter but not the spirit of the decision, that the decision can produce attitude change inconsistent with policy goals, and that law recipients, though they may have a cognitive understanding of their rights under a judicial decision, frequently have no appreciation of them nor an ability to apply them. The pattern of compliance with what some would call the "repressive" legal norm of censorship appears to be the same as with the allegedly "liberating" norms of *Miranda* and the other criminal justice cases referred to above, at least according to one study of bookseller practices. In this study, James P. Levine, examined the short-run effects of *Ginzburg v. United States*,[35] a restrictive obscenity decision. Levine found that although nearly an entire year had passed since the Court's decision, only 5 percent of the sample of booksellers had made any changes in their policies or practices as a direct result of *Ginzburg*, and that those changes which were made were minor in scope. "The influence of *Ginzburg* on the dissemination of sex literature in the general bookstore has been minuscule."[36]

If it is difficult to determine the impact of a judicial decision on the behavior of law appliers and recipients, it is apparently even more difficult to assess its impact on their attitudes. We do have some reason to believe that there is considerable attitudinal support for at least the U.S. Supreme Court, generally, resting upon a limited understanding of what the Court does.[37] And, William K. Muir's recent study of the school prayer decisions and attitude change has shown that law does have some capacity to change deep rooted attitudes.[38]

However, there are at least two reasons why we cannot yet conclude with reasonable certainty that legal decisions can change the attitudes of law appliers and recipients, even in the long run. First, most of the data we have accumulated on the question up to now rests on some variety of survey research, and no matter how sophisticated we may have become with survey research techniques we cannot always distinguish between true support and lip service. Second, even Muir points out that the attitudinal change he found was clearly dependent upon the individual's personality and environmental experiences. It just may be that in those instances where the legal decision applies to a particular jurisdiction where opposition to it is nearly unanimous, entrenched, and based upon strong emotion, it will have practically no effect upon attitudes whatsoever; or, if it does, a countereffect.

COURTS AND POLICY PROBLEMS

In this chapter we have examined the potential utility of the legal system in the resolution of political problems. It is time now to catalogue its advantages and limitations in this regard.

Let us begin with its advantages.

(1) The judiciary provides an alternative and often acquiescent forum for seeking solutions to political problems when the participants in the legislative process are either unwilling or unable to act. Judges, as opposed to policy makers in the legislative and executive branches, are more nearly, or at least more often, removed from the current clash of competing interests, more insulated from political pressures. Thus, they are more likely to do what is right even if such action alienates powerful individuals or incurs the wrath of vested interests or is otherwise politically disadvantageous. This is particularly true when the judges are appointed rather than elected as is the case with all national judges and many state judges. But even when elected, judges tend to possess a habit of mind (often called "judicial temperament") which allows them to rise above the demands of partisan politics. To be sure, this posture and insulation may lead them to ignore rather than acquiesce in the demands of political reformers if their judicial role requires it. But in the same sense, and probably to a greater extent, judges will ignore the opponents of

reform if the laws or the Constitution require it. In support of this argument, we might cite the initiative and leadership successfully assumed by the courts in such problem areas as school desegregation and legislative reapportionment. Further, there is growing reason to believe that the courts will take the policy initiative in such currently difficult issues as consumer protection and environmental defense.

(2) Judge-made law as opposed to legislatively enacted law possesses a greater relative legitimacy. At first glance, of course, the opposite would appear to be true. After all, the legislative branch is supposed to be the representative mechanism through which the legitimizing criterion of majority rule is operationalized. The judiciary, on the other hand, is not supposed to make law at all but merely find and interpret it. But precisely herein lies the judiciary's policy-making potential. The citizenry is often inclined to believe, usually correctly, that laws emanating from the legislative branch are the products of bargaining, compromise, logrolling, or porkbarrel (all of which is summed up in the negative connotation of the characteristic word "deals"), thus not conforming to majority rule anyway. The judiciary, however, need not meet this requirement because its job is not to represent the people but simply to interpret the laws in such a way as to conform with the dictates of precedent and the fundamental charter, the Constitution. To preserve their legitimacy the courts need only produce the appearance of being fair, objective, and bound down generally by the requirements of due process. Their alleged insulation from politics gives the courts what some have called a mystic power, the capacity to generate support for their decisions largely on the popular belief that they were arrived at on the basis of neutrality in the antiseptic environment of the courtroom.

Perhaps the most dramatic example of this mystic power can be found in the reaction to the Supreme Court's decision in the famous school desegregation case of *Brown v. Board of Education*,[39] in which it was decided that separate schools for the two races, even if equal, are not permissible in principle. Although that decision was rendered in 1954, the Court did not issue a decree making things happen commensurate with the decision for nearly a year. This was because, the Court said, the formulation of decrees in these kinds of cases "presents problems of considerable complexity." Nevertheless, by early 1955, although there had been as yet no command from the court forcing things to happen, more than 500 school districts, involving some 250,000 black pupils, had abandoned policies of segregation. Although it represented only a small percentage of all segregated districts, and although the Court was still obligated to issue a decree, this unrequired movement toward integration was "a demonstration of the spell the Court is capable of casting, a manifestation of its prestige, of the force of its mystique, and of the dominion of ideas."[40]

There is one obvious weakness in this mystic power, however, which cannot be overemphasized. That weakness is that courts cannot rely on it too frequently or they will lose the very image of legitimacy upon which the power is based. As those judges who believe in a more restrained role for courts commonly point out, the power of courts rests almost exclusively upon sustained public confidence which must be nourished by avoiding political controversy. If the citizenry should develop the notion that judges possess an unlimited discretion in making public policy, the courts will lose what little influence they already have. Without the power of the purse or the sword, courts depend heavily upon their image, accurate or not, as unbiased instruments of justice. The more they are relied upon as political instruments, the less legitimate they will become.

This leads us into a consideration of the limitations on utilizing the legal system for problem solving.

(1) One limitation is inherent in the constraints produced by those values of judges, those "process ideas," which lead them to refuse to involve themselves with political problems. Lumped together these ideas are often called the elements of judicial self-restraint, the justification for which is usually articulated as above in the context of legitimacy. Not all of these elements are directly relevant to our analysis, but let us mention a few which are. First, there is the so-called political questions doctrine, according to which courts should not interfere with the discretionary authority of the other agencies of government. This, in short, is the notion that there exist some types of questions which are "not meet for judicial determination." Although a number of judges have offered definitions of a political question, none has developed a suitable formula for distinguishing between a political question and a legal one. As a result, "Political questions are those which judges choose not to decide, and a question becomes political by the judge's refusal to decide it."[41] Hence, some questions once considered political and therefore not answered by courts have since received judicial treatment and are thus no longer considered political (such as the problem of legislative apportionment). It does not matter, however, whether a judge truly subscribes to the political questions doctrine generally and across the board or whether he invokes

it only in particular instances to protect his personal political goals. The fact still remains that the doctrine can be a formidable obstacle to those who would use the legal system to advance a political cause. And as the most recent experiences with reapportionment have taught us, there might indeed be some instances in which the courts ought to stay out of the thicket.

A second element of restraint is the notion that courts ought not formulate rules of law broader than required by the precise facts to which they are to be applied. This means that unless the problem solver can present to the courts in an adversary situation an issue which can be worded in such a manner as to elicit a judicial response which specifically answers the question he has in mind, he cannot count on the courts for help. This norm is related to yet a third element of restraint, which is that courts will not render decisions in friendly, nonadversary proceedings. There must be at hand a concrete case and controversy. Such a requirement raises the entire question of accessibility to the court which involves a whole new range of obstacles constituting the second limitation to using the courts for problem solving.

(2) The judicial process establishes quite restrictive conditions on the availability of court action. We have already suggested that the courts are passive in nature. That is, even if they wish to solve a specific political problem they must wait in inactive receptivity until a case that raises that particular question is brought properly before them. The term "properly" suggests a second restrictive condition—a court must have jurisdiction over a conflict before it can settle it. Third, courts often depend on other government agencies for many of their powers. They are often at the mercy of the other branches and cannot afford to alienate them. The most dramatic example of this limitation is the Supreme Court's total dependence upon Congress for its appellate jurisdiction.[42]

(3) There is often no source of constitutional or statutory authority upon which the adjudication of political issues can be based, and the more the legal system is used to solve political problems the more scarce these sources will become. This is the argument that courts are beginning to exhaust their sources of authority when dealing with political problems. It does not deny that courts have made significant changes in the recent past in such areas as reapportionment, civil rights, and consumer protection. However, as Chief Justice Warren E. Burger recently pointed out, those decisions resulted from "the application of long available constitutional guarantees to existing situations not previously presented

to the courts. . . . For the most part, it was legislation flowing from the political process that was the source of the progress we sometimes credit to judges."[43] Hence, if we want to use the courts to solve political problems, we must sometimes stimulate (or otherwise rely upon) the legislative and administrative process to provide us with a broader range of authority upon which to act. We must realize that courts are already overburdened with litigation, and that the more the legal system is used the less persuasive is the argument that, as opposed to the legislature, courts provide a forum for action to which access is easier and from which results are speedier. Indeed, lengthy delays and other defects in judicial administration must clearly detract from the contributions courts can make to resolving political problems. It is true that a number of steps have been taken in recent years to reduce court delay. However, backlogs continue and thus court delay itself is a current political problem which must be solved.

Unquestionably, the litigation process can be an effective tool for achieving political change. Sometimes it provides a viable alternative to problem solvers frustrated by the political process. And, almost always, judicial decisions are viewed by those to whom they are applied as more "just" and/or "legitimate" than legislative enactments. But ultimately, the judiciary depends on the political process for its authority, and nearly every advantage that the judiciary possesses for problem solving can be destroyed if used too often. Adjudication can be a cruel, costly, clumsy, and sluggish instrument for change, unless we are satisfied in measuring change in terms of decades, or even lifetimes. Further, judges and lawyers are inhibited by their own legal style in policy making, the consequences of which were discussed in chapter 5.

In conclusion, however, we ought to avoid complete disparagement of the legal style in policy making. There is much to admire in the rise of "Naderism," in the rational application of multi-dimensional, reformist standards within the litigation-appeal context and under the compelling auspices of the "reasonable man" concept. But the ultimate dilemma is this: The law, as an instrument for change is limited by its own unchanging modes of growth; it must rely on a limited stock of concepts which inhibit the development of new ideas enhancing social change.[44] The law itself faces no greater challenge than when called upon to redistribute societal values. All of which may be to conclude simply that the law is not nearly so much an instrument for achieving change as it is an instrument for achieving accommodation between change and stability.

9

JURISPRUDENCE AND JURISCIENCE

The general thesis advanced in this book is that: (1) jurisprudence was the first of the social sciences and as a precursory discipline (from roughly 1800 to 1900) it provided the newly emerging social sciences with data, methods, and tools which assisted their subsequent development and for which they became intellectually indebted; (2) slowly (by roughly 1930–50), the richness of jurisprudence as a source of data and theory declined but the modern social sciences were not yet sufficiently developed methodologically to assist the continued advancement of scholarly knowledge about law; and (3) in the decades of the 1960s and 70s the modern social scientific study of law has begun to pay off on its debt to jurisprudence by answering questions it had left unanswered and thereby has started to become an emerging juriscience. We must insert the adjective "emerging" because the term "juriscience" unadorned would misleadingly suggest that a thoroughly scientific framework had already produced a general theory of law. The fact is that we are still in a theory-building stage. Quantified and operational propositions have been set down and partial theories have emerged but no complete, general theory of law has been produced. Also, juriscience (and the other modern social sciences) is now in a postbehavioral stage in which the exclusive thrust toward value-free inquiry has been abandoned. That is not to say that postbehavioralism is identical with traditionalism or conventionalism in which normative inquiry predominated, but that modern research technology is now used to study values as well as other social phenomenon.

In chapter 1, we recognize that the original and etymological meaning of the term "jurisprudence" is the science of law. But we also recognize that the word "science" in this context is used in the classical Greek sense and does not include a modern social science component. Thus, the jurisprudential heritage of the contemporary student of legal process and policy making, is directly traceable no further back than to about the year 1800 when the German historicists and English positivists carved out a distinct sphere of intellectual concerns centered nearly exclusively in the law as a unique phenomenon. We define jurisprudence then as the sociological analysis of the concepts and rules which legal systems develop and legal actors apply and of the social interests which law protects. As such, jurisprudence constructed by the 1950s a social scientific foundation (which the modern social sciences have built upon in the 1960s and 1970s) by explaining judicial behavior and the judicial policy-making method. As described in detail at the end of chapter 2, that jurisprudential foundation consisted of, specifically, the search for an objective, value-free science, an emphasis on statistics and statistical analyses, the discovery of the subconscious judicial mind, and an emphasis on precise empirical analysis, careful conceptualization, and rigorous classification. It is true that in the early nineteenth century the famous mathematician Marquis de Laplace had applied probability theory to the number of judges required in a tribunal in order that "error probability," as he called it, would be tolerably small.[1] So even the realist school of jurisprudence had its precursor in this narrow sense. But in the broader context of assumption and approach, it is the discipline of jurisprudence, not isolated developments in other disciplines, which laid the foundation for the social scientific study of legal process.

Today we are approaching the existence of a juriscience. By juriscience we mean the modern social scientific study of law assisted by a new research technology as it has evolved over the last two decades to answer questions jurisprudence left unanswered because of its methodological limitations. Juriscience includes (but is much broader in substance) than jurimetrics, which usually refers to the quantitative study of judicial decision making. The broad substantive canvass of juriscience includes private law as well as public law, civil justice policy as well as criminal justice policy, and policy-making dynamics as well as structural and behavioral dynamics. Indeed, some scholars now appear willing to regard the social scientific study of law as sufficiently advanced to constitute a subcomponent of juridical policy science.[2] Clearly, over the last two decades, there has been a reversal in the direction of contributions flowing between jurisprudence and juriscience, with jurisprudence now receiving more contributions than it makes. Although the basic distinction between jurisprudence and juriscience is methodological not conceptual, the newer research methods have produced findings which have led in turn to changing conceptions about law and legal process and to a broader subject-matter canvass. Juriscience first emerged in the 1950s and early 1960s as jurimetrics, and at that point answered only one of the many questions left unanswered by jurisprudence—the question of judicial method (labeled by jurimetrics as "judicial behavior"). By the mid 1970s, however, juriscience has broadened its scope so as to address a widened range of jurisprudential concerns.

In this book we have not attempted to synthesize all of these contributions but only to suggest what light juriscience has shed on the courts and their actors as policy makers. After identifying our subject matter as the process of authoritatively allocating justice as a valued end, we proceed with a juriscientific description of structural, behavioral and policy-making dynamics.

In structural terms, we find an American judiciary arranged around the principle of federalism, itself a largely legal dimension or variable with impact on public policy.[3] In this context we find that one structural dynamic is that state court judges, striving to preserve their independence from the national judiciary, are much more likely to cite precedents from the courts of other states than from national courts when they can find no precise authority in point in their own state's laws. State court judges are particularly reluctant to cite U.S. Supreme Court rulings. Further, structural duality creates a strategic environment in which litigants "shop" for the most attractive forum and there is considerable evidence that different forums produce different outcomes, especially when state courts strive to evade U.S. Supreme Court decisions. In terms of the politics of administering the structure of courts we find that: (1) policy considerations (rather than the goal of greater efficiency) commonly motivate inter-circuit assignments of the Federal Judicial Conference; (2) Federal Judicial Conference policies allow national courts, in effect, to give advisory opinions because as an agency of the national judiciary the conference can speak with authority, thus producing policy through an administrative rather than an adversary process; and (3) judges sometimes use the politics of judicial administration to (a) speak out on issues which later reach them as concrete cases, and (b) promote their professional status. Finally, we find that although differing judicial selection mechanisms generate differing sets of informal qualifications and involve the political participation of differing groups, the politics of judicial selection is not directly related to either the quality of the law school the judicial candidate attended, or his qualifications as measured by prior experience or his decision-making style.

In behavioral terms, we are now better able to identify and measure the relative weights of the various determinants of the judicial decision. Although some of the correlations are statistically weak, we find that discrete backgrounds (in terms of family and class, prior professional experience, party affiliation, religion, and other life experiences) are related to judicial decision-making tendencies. Attributes influence and filter through the complex interactions between values, role perceptions, and bloc activity to produce a result—judicial decision or other strategic behavior—that is not unassociated with the character of the attributes themselves. We know more about these complex interactions because we have devised tools to study values, role perceptions and bloc activity and are now able to measure the relative weights of legal facts and personal values as they combine to produce judicial behavior. We can say that it is the association of factual stimulus and precedent with a judge's previous typical attitudes that determine his behavior, that is, the facts of a case fix its position on the judge's value scale and it is this position which determines his vote.

Some advances have also been made in explaining the behavior of other participants in the legal process. The legal style in policy making by lawyers (in judicial and nonjudicial arenas) sets narrow limits on the data they consider and on the remedies they propose and this style is a principal determinant of incremental process and substance in policy making. Further, the interorganizational exchange model can now help explain the discretionary arrest behavior of police, the discretionary charge behavior of prosecutors, and the discretionary sentencing behavior of judges in criminal justice policy. A similar approach to civil justice policy has also been productive and is consistent with the contemporary policy focus of much social science research.

In these policy-making terms, juriscience can now comment meaningfully on the relationship between law and social change. We know more than ever before about the strategies and mechanisms for obtaining favorable court decisions (or outputs). And we are increasingly able to measure their impact (or outcomes). Although the findings are divided, we can say, generally, that (1) the analysis of law and social change must distinguish between changes in behavior (the immediate objective) and changes in attitudes (a more remote and long-term achievement); (2) judicial decisions can produce attitude changes inconsistent with policy objectives, though in some areas judicial decisions do seem to have demonstrated some capacity to change, in a favorable direction, even deep-rooted attitudes; (3) law recipients (those who theoretically neither make nor apply decisions but benefit from them) may have a cognitive understanding of their rights under a judicial decision but frequently have no appreciation of them nor an ability to use them; and (4) although there are both advantages and limitations to using the courts to solve policy problems, the judiciary is probably not so much an instrument for change as it is an instrument for accommodating between change and stability. Admittedly, juriscience as a body of data and theoretical knowledge has not yet developed sufficiently to produce a "juridical policy science," that is, it has not developed sufficiently to be of certain and consistent assistance to policy makers. Yehezkel Dror does not want a formal juridical subdiscipline of policy science (as a holistic approach to policy making) anyway.[4] But he does think that law should be (and that it increasingly is) considered a policy-sciences-related discipline and social institution. Law, to Dror, is both a tool for normative policy analysis and (among its other social functions) a social policy instrument.[5] He concludes, "The growing use of law as an instrument of organized societal direction seems to be one of the characteristics of modern society."[6] Juriscience is beginning to contribute to such a policy sciences perspective.

Certainly, much more remains to be done. In political science the continued study of formal structures and of the behavior of legal actors in both judicial and nonjudicial arenas can tell us much more than we now know about the determinants of public policy. In sociology the relationship between law and social change must be subjected to more careful inquiry. In anthropology ethnographic studies can tell us much more about not only the sources of law but also about the perceptions and shared knowledge of actors in trial courts. In psychology research can help us better explain such legal constructs as "intent," "negligence," "recklessness," and "accident." To be sure, those of us in juriscience (which is probably a subdiscipline in all of the social sciences) continue to quibble over methods. Although the interface between law and society is receiving more and more scholarly attention (as evidenced by the emergence and popularity of such publications as *The Law and Society Review*), there continue to be differences between the way lawyers and social scientists approach the subject matter. Social scientists are generally more eager to carve out boundaries and develop models for testing while lawyers are far more willing to examine all the data they can find and determine what they can make of it.[7] And the policy implementation of juriscience, proceeding as it must in lock-step fashion with the evolution of quantitative forms of measurement,[8] must await the appearance of an even more methodologically sophisticated approach to law. Certainly, lawyers must be involved in this scholarly process, but what has been accomplished in juriscience to date, at a minimum, is that we need no longer fear that the study of law will be left exclusively to lawyers.

NOTES

1. JURISPRUDENCE AND SOCIAL SCIENCE

1. For a more complete survey of the various usages of jurisprudence see George Whitecross Paton, *Jurisprudence* (London: Oxford University Press, 1951), pp. 1-4, and Roscoe Pound, "Jurisprudence," *Encyclopedia of the Social Sciences*, 8, edited by Edwin Seligman (New York: The Macmillan Co., 1932), pp. 477-92.

2. Pound, p. 477.

3. Paton, p. 2.

4. Pound, p. 477.

5. Jerome Hall, "Unification of Political and Legal Theory," *Political Science Quarterly* 69 (March, 1954): 15-16.

6. Pound, p. 477.

7. Savigny's principal work is *Of the Vocation of Our Age for Legislation and Jurisprudence,* translated by Abraham Hayward (London: University of London Press, 1931).

8. Ernest Barker, "Introduction to Gierke, Natural Law and the Theory of Society," in *Readings in Jurisprudence,* edited by Jerome Hall (Indianapolis: Bobbs-Merrill Co., 1938), pp. 91-92.

39. Paton, pp. 14-17.

10. Austin's principal work is *The Province of Jurisprudence Determined* (London: University of London Press, 1842).

11. Paton, p. 6.

12. Pound, p. 481.

13. Wolfgang Friedmann, *Legal Theory,* 3rd ed. (London: Stevens and Sons, Ltd., 1953), p. 163.

14. Paton, pp. 8-9, 168-69.

15. Rudolf von Jhering, *The Struggle for Law,* translated by John J. Lalor (Chicago: Callaghan and Co., 1879), p. 1.

16. Ibid., pp. 1-2.

17. Paton, p. 17.

18. Pound's leading works are *An Introduction to the Philosophy of Law* (New Haven: Yale University Press, 1922), *Law and Morals* (Chapel Hill: University of North Carolina Press, 1924), and *Social Control through Law* (New Haven: Yale University Press, 1942).

19. Paton, p. 18.
20. Eugen Ehrlich, *Fundamental Principles of the Sociology of Law,* translated by W. L. Moll (Cambridge: Harvard University Press, 1936), p. 488.
21. Pound, "Jurisprudence," *Encyclopedia of the Social Sciences,* p. 484.
22. Paton, p. 18.
23. Oliver Wendell Holmes, Jr., *The Common Law* (Boston: Little, Brown and Co., 1938), p. 1 (published originally in 1881).
24. Ibid.
25. Holmes, "The Path of the Law," *Harvard Law Review* 10 (1897): 457.
26. See Benjamin N. Cardozo, *The Nature of the Judicial Process* (New Haven: Yale University Press, 1921) and *The Paradoxes of Legal Science* (New York: Columbia University Press, 1928).
27. Paton, p. 19.
28. Karl N. Llewellyn, "Some Realism about Realism," *Harvard Law Review* 44 (1931): 1222–64.
29. Glendon Schubert (ed.), *Judicial Behavior: A Reader in Theory and Research* (Chicago: Rand McNally & Co., 1964), p. 11.
30. Ibid.
31. Llewellyn's leading work is *Jurisprudence: Realism in Theory and Practice* (Chicago: University of Chicago Press, 1962); Frank's principal work is *Law and the Modern Mind* (New York: Tudor Publishing Co., 1936).
32. Kelsen's leading works are *The General Theory of Law and State* (Cambridge: Harvard University Press, 1945) and *The Pure Theory of Law,* translated by Max Knight (Berkeley: University of California Press, 1967).
33. Paton, pp. 10–14.
34. Ibid., p. 13.
35. Ibid.
36. Alf Ross, *On Law and Justice* (Berkeley: University of California Press, 1967).

2. ANTHROPOLOGY OF LAW

1. See William Seagle, *The Quest for Law* (New York: Alfred A. Knopf, 1941), p. 5. Much of my analysis of definitions and typology follows Seagle closely.
2. George Whitecross Paton, *Jurisprudence* (London: Oxford University Press, 1951), pp. 52–54.
3. Ibid., pp. 54–55.
4. Seagle, pp. 5–7.
5. Ibid., pp. 27–35.
6. Ibid., p. 35.
7. Ibid.
8. Paton, p. 36.
9. Seagle, pp. 63–65.
10. Ibid., p. 69.
11. Sir John Salmond, *Jurisprudence* (London: Sweet and Maxwell, Ltd., 1920), p. 13.
12. Francis R. Aumann, *The Instrumentalities of Justice: Their Forms, Functions, and Limitations* (Columbus, Ohio: The Ohio State University Press, 1956), p. 3.
13. Sir Henry Maine, *Ancient Law* (New York: Henry Holt and Co., 1885), p. 25.
14. Paton, pp. 43–44.
15. Seagle, p. 151.
16. Paton, pp. 182–205.
17. Seagle, pp. 277–98.
18. Ibid., pp. 180–81.

19. Ibid., p. xv.
20. Paton, pp. 182–85.
21. Justice Felix Frankfurter in *Terminiello v. Chicago,* 337 U.S. 1 (1949).
22. *The Federalist Papers,* No. 78, New American Library edition, p. 471.
23. See Walter F. Murphy, *Elements of Judicial Strategy* (Chicago: University of Chicago Press, 1964), p. 1.
24. Wallace Mendelson, "The Neo-Behavioral Approach to the Judicial Process: A Critique," *American Political Science Review* 57 (1963): 603.
25. Paton, p. 150.
26. Benjamin N. Cardozo, *The Nature of the Judicial Process* (New Haven: Yale University Press, 1921). My summary is taken from the following pages: 9–10, 112–15, 170–72.
27. Ibid., pp. 112–13.
28. Ibid., p. 115.
29. Ibid., p. 170.
30. Ibid.
31. Ibid., p. 12.
32. See Huntington Cairns, *Law and the Social Sciences* (New York: Harcourt, Brace & Co., 1935) and *Theory of Legal Science* (Chapel Hill: University of North Carolina Press, 1941).

3. THE ARENA

1. Article III, section 1.
2. Herbert Jacob, *Justice in America* (Boston: Little, Brown and Company, 1972), pp. 145–46.
3. Article VI, section 2.
4. Wheaton 304 (1816).
5. Stuart Nagel, "Sociometric Relations among American Courts," *Southwest Social Science Quarterly* 43 (1962): 136–42.
6. Note, "State Court Evasion of United States Supreme Court Mandates," *Yale Law Journal* 56 (1947): 574–83.
7. Henry J. Abraham, *The Judiciary* (Boston: Allyn and Bacon, Inc., 1973), pp. 3–4.
8. Charles R. Adrian, *State and Local Governments* (New York: McGraw-Hill, 1976), p. 343.
9. Abraham, p. 4.
10. Adrian, p. 343.
11. Morris Ploscowe, "The Inferior Criminal Courts in Action," *Annals* 287 (1953): 8–12.
12. Alfred Steinbert, "The Small Claims Court: A Consumer's Forgotten Forum," *National Civic Review* 63 (1974): 289 ff.
13. Herbert Jacob, *Urban Justice* (Englewood Cliffs, New Jersey: Prentice-Hall Inc., 1973), pp. 86–87.
14. Abraham, p. 5.
15. Jacob, *Justice in America,* pp. 150–51.
16. Ibid., p. 151.
17. Robert J. Sickels, "The Illusion of Judicial Consensus," *American Political Science Review* 59 (1965): 100–104.
18. Joel B. Grossman, *Lawyers and Judges: The ABA and the Politics of Judicial Selection* (New York: John Wiley & Sons, 1965).
19. R. Eric Weise and Alfred de Grazia, *Eight Branches: American Government Today* (Columbus, Ohio: Collegiate Publishing, Inc., 1975), p. 321.
20. Glendon Schubert, *Constitutional Politics* (New York: Holt, Rinehart & Winston, 1960), p. 100.

21. See United States Code, chapter 81, title 28, section 1254.
22. Abraham, pp. 6–8.
23. Jacob, *Justice in America*, pp. 153–54.
24. Will Shafroth, "Modern Developments in Judicial Administration," *American University Law Review* 12 (1963): 153–56.
25. Jay A. Sigler, *An Introduction to the Legal System* (Homewood, Illinois: Dorsey Press, 1968), pp. 75–76.
26. Peter Graham Fish, *The Politics of Federal Judicial Administration* (Princeton, New Jersey: Princeton University Press, 1973), pp. 436–37.
27. See Peter Westen, "The Proposed National Court of Appeals: A Threat to the Supreme Court," *Law Quadrangle News* 17 (1973): 12–17.
28. John Stookey, "The Certiorari Decision in the U.S. Supreme Court," a paper prepared for delivery at the 1975 Midwest Political Science Association Convention at Chicago, Illinois; May 1–3, 1975.
29. Herbert Jacob and Kenneth Vines, *Politics in the American States* (Boston: Little, Brown & Co., 1976), p. 248.
30. Council of State Governments, *State Court Systems* (Chicago: Council of State Governments, 1970), pp. 70–71.
31. Jacob, *Justice in America*, p. 154.
32. Ibid., p. 155.

4. JUDGES AND JUDICIAL DECISION

1. Herbert Jacob and Kenneth N. Vines, *Politics in the American States* (Boston: Little, Brown & Co., 1976), p. 249.
2. James Herndon, "Appointment as a Means of Initial Accession to State Courts of Last Resort," *North Dakota Law Review* 38 (1962): 60–73.
3. Carl D. McMurray and Malcom B. Parsons, "Public Attitudes toward the Representational Role of Legislators and Judges," *Midwest Journal of Political Science* 9 (1965): 167–85.
4. Jack Ladinsky and Alan Silver, "Popular Democracy and Judicial Independence," *Wisconsin Law Review* 71.
5. Burton M. Atkins and Henry R. Glick, "Formal Judicial Recruitment and State Supreme Court Decisions," *American Politics Quarterly* 2 (1974): 427–49.
6. Richard A. Watson and Ronald G. Downing, *The Politics of the Bench and the Bar: Judicial Selection under the Missouri Nonpartisan Court Plan* (New York: John Wiley, 1969), pp. 338–39.
7. Bradley Cannon, "The Impact of Formal Selection Processes on the Characteristics of Judges," *Law and Society Review* 6 (1972): 579–93.
8. Jacob and Vines, pp. 252–53.
9. Ibid.
10. Henry J. Abraham, *The Judiciary* (Boston: Allyn and Bacon, 1973), p. 16, n. 7.
11. The best account of the selection of national judges prior to the Nixon years is Joel B. Grossman, *Lawyers and Judges: The ABA and the Politics of Judicial Selection* (New York: John Wiley, 1965).
12. William C. Louthan, *Mr. Justice Wiley Rutledge and Questions of Public Policy: A Study of Discretion and Objectivity in Judicial Decision-Making* (Columbus, Ohio: unpublished Ph.D. dissertation, Ohio State University, 1970), pp. 49–71.
13. Robert Dahl, "Decision-Making in a Democracy: The Supreme Court as a National Policy Maker," *Journal of Public Law* 6 (1958): 280–92.
14. Herbert Jacob, "The Effect of Institutional Differences in the Recruitment Process: The Case of State Judges," *Journal of Public Law* 13 (1964): 104–19.

15. Herbert Jacob, *Justice in America* (Boston: Little, Brown and Co., 1972), p. 107.
16. Jacob and Vines, p. 249.
17. Lou Cannon, *Ronnie and Jesse: A Political Odyssey* (Garden City, New York: Doubleday & Co., 1969), p. 303.
18. Charles Adrian, *State and Local Governments* (New York: McGraw-Hill, 1976), p. 356.
19. Jacob and Vines, p. 250.
20. Ibid.
21. Jacob, *Justice in America*, p. 97.
22. Walter F. Murphy, *Elements of Judicial Strategy* (Chicago: University of Chicago Press, 1964).
23. Murphy, *Elements of Judicial Strategy*, pp. 37, 43, 73–78.
24. Charles Fairman, *Mr. Justice Miller and the Supreme Court, 1862-1890* (Cambridge: Harvard Press, 1939), pp. 349–68.
25. Willard L. King, *Melville Weston Fuller* (New York: Macmillan, 1950), pp. 180–81.
26. Taft's role is described particularly well in David Danelski, *A Supreme Court Justice Is Appointed* (New York: Random House, 1964) with respect to the appointment of Justice Pierce Butler.
27. See chapter 3, "The Politics of Appointment" in Louthan, pp. 60–65.
28. S. Sidney Ulmer, "The Political Party Variable in the Michigan Supreme Court," *Journal of Public Law* 11 (1962), 352–62.
29. Walter F. Murphy and Joseph Tanenhaus, *The Study of Public Law* (New York: Random House, 1972), pp. 110–11.
30. Murphy, *Elements of Judicial Strategy*, pp. 1–11.
31. Louthan, pp. 181–82.
32. J. Woodford Howard, *Mr. Justice Murphy: A Political Biography* (Princeton, Princeton University Press, 1968), pp. 346, 481–88.
33. (New York: Macmillan, 1948).
34. Charles H. Sheldon, *The American Judicial Process* (New York: Dodd, Mead, & Co., 1974).
35. John R. Schmidhouser, "The Justices of the Supreme Court: A Collective Portrait," *Midwest Journal of Political Science* 3 (1959): 45.
36. Grossman, pp. 19–20.
37. Murphy and Tanenhaus, p. 99.
38. Jacob, *Justice in America*, pp. 116–17.
39. John R. Schmidhauser, *Constitutional Law in the Political Process* (Chicago: Rand McNally, 1963), pp. 511–12.
40. Ibid., pp. 512–13.
41. Stuart Nagel, "Political Party Affiliation and Judges' Decisions," *American Political Science Review* 55 (1961): 843; and Nagel, "Testing Relations between Judicial Characteristics and Judicial Decision Making," *Western Political Quarterly* 15 (1962): 425.
42. See summary in Jacob, *Justice in America*, pp. 117–18.
43. Stuart Nagel, "Judicial Backgrounds and Criminal Cases," *Journal of Criminal Law, Criminology, and Police Science* 53 (1962): 335.
44. Sheldon Goldman, "Voting Behavior on the United States Courts of Appeals 1961-1964," *American Political Science Review* 60 (1966): 374.
45. Sheldon Goldman and Thomas P. Jahnige, *The Federal Courts as a Political System* (New York: Harper & Row, 1976), p. 160.
46. Harold J. Spaeth, *An Introduction to Supreme Court Decision Making* (San Francisco: Chandler, 1972), pp. 64–66.
47. Ibid., p. 61.
48. 328 U.S. 549 (1946).
49. Louthan, pp. 162–63.

50.   Glendon Schubert, *Constitutional Politics* (New York: Holt, Rinehart and Winston, 1960), p. 155.

51.   Ibid., p. 109.

52.   Ibid., pp. 108–10.

53.   (New York: Macmillan, 1948).

54.   (Chicago: University of Chicago Press, 1954).

55.   *Vinson Court*, p. 191.

56.   *Roosevelt Court*, pp. 41–43, 240–53; *Vinson Court*, pp. 190–92.

57.   David N. Atkinson and Dale A. Neuman, "Toward a Cost Theory of Judicial Alignments: The Case of the Truman Bloc," *Midwest Journal of Political Science* 13 (1969): 271–83.

58.   Ibid., p. 275.

59.   See David W. Rohde, "Comments on a Cost Theory of Judicial Alignments," *Midwest Journal of Political Science* 14 (1960): 331–36.

60.   Werner F. Grumbaum, "Analytical and Simulation Models for Explaining Judicial Decision-Making" in *Frontiers of Judicial Research*, edited by Joel B. Grossman and Joseph Tanenhaus (New York: Wiley, 1969), pp. 315–16.

61.   393 U.S. 23 (1968).

62.   Grumbaum, "A Quantitative Analysis of the 'Presidential Ballot' Case," *Journal of Politics* 34 (1972): 221–43.

5. LAWYERS AND LEGAL STYLE

1.   Frederick G. Kempin, Jr., *Historical Introduction to Anglo-American Law* (St. Paul, Minnesota: West Publishing Co., 1973), pp. 65–67.

2.   Ibid., pp. 67–68.

3.   Herbert Jacob, *Justice in America* (Boston: Little, Brown and Co., 1972), pp. 46–51.

4.   Ibid., pp. 44–46, 50–51.

5.   Francis R. Aumann, *The Instrumentalities of Justice* (Columbus: The Ohio State University Press, 1956), pp. 96–97.

6.   Much of this section is adapted from an unpublished article which I co-authored with Carl Akins entitled "The Legal Style in Policy-Making" (Washington, D.C.: American University, 1972).

7.   Aumann, p. 90.

8.   Ibid., pp. 109–21.

9.   See, for example: Heinz Eulau and John Sprague, *Lawyers in Politics: A Study Professional Convergence* (Indianapolis: Bobbs-Merrill, 1964); Wayne V. McIntosh and John E. Stanga, Jr., "Lawyers and Political Participation," *Journal of Politics* 8 (1976): 434–41; and James A. Dyer, "Do Lawyers Vote Differently? A Study of voting on No-Fault Insurance," *Journal of Politics* 38 (1976): 452–56.

10.   Dyer, p. 455.

11.   David R. Derge, "The Lawyer as Decision-Maker in the American State Legislature," *Journal of Politics* 21 (1959): 408–33; and Derge, "The Lawyer in the Indiana General Assembly," *Midwest Journal of Political Science* 6 (1962): 19–53.

12.   Eulau and Sprague, pp. 22–27.

13.   McIntosh and Stanga, 440–41.

14.   George Whitecross Paton, *Jurisprudence* (London: Oxford University Press, 1951), pp. 150–52, 166, 168.

15.   Ralph Nader, "Law Schools and Law Firms," *Minnesota Law Review* 54 (1970): 493–502.

16.   Ibid., pp. 493–94.

17.   Ibid.

18.   Edwin W. Tucker, *Adjudication of Social Issues* (St. Paul, Minnesota: West Publishing Co., 1971), p. 40.

19.   199 Okla. 369, 371 (1947).
20.   James E. Krier, *Environmental Law and Policy* (Indianapolis: Bobbs-Merrill, 1971), p. 185.
21.   Ibid., pp. 187–88.
22.   *Hulbert v. California Portland Cement Co.*, 161 Cal. 239 (1911).
23.   Krier, p. 188.
24.   Ibid., p. 235.
25.   262 U.S. 447 (1923).
26.   392 U.S. 83 (1968).
27.   Tucker, p. 40.
28.   401 U.S. 907 (1971).
29.   J. H. Dales, *Pollution, Property and Prices* (Toronto: University of Toronto Press, 1968), pp. 88-93.
30.   Krier, p. 468.
31.   William Seagle, *The Quest for Law* (New York: Alfred A. Knopf, 1941), pp. 91-101.

6. CRIMINAL JUSTICE POLICY

1.   Congressional Quarterly Service, *Crime and the Law* (Washington, D.C.: Congressional Quarterly, 1971), pp. 1–6.
2.   Herbert Jacob, *Justice in America* (Boston: Little, Brown and Co., 1972), pp. 164–77.
3.   Macklin Fleming, *The Price of Perfect Justice* (New York: Basic Books, 1974), pp. 15-50.
4.   Winfield S. Bollinger and Karl O. Vezner, "Intergovernmental Relations and Criminal Justice," paper prepared for delivery at the 1974 Annual Meeting of the American Political Science Association at Chicago, Illinois; August 29–September 2, 1974.
5.   William C. Louthan, "Relationships among Police, Court and Correctional Agencies," *Policy Studies Journal* 3 (1974): 30–37. (Much of the next section is adapted from this article.)
6.   William M. Evan, "Towards a Theory of Inter-Organizational Relations," *Management Science* 11 (August, 1965): 218–30.
7.   George F. Cole, "The Decision to Prosecute," *Law and Society Review* 4 (February, 1970): 313–43.
8.   Ibid., pp. 313-17.
9.   John Kaplan, *Criminal Justice* (Mineola, N.Y.: The Foundation Press, 1973), p. 70.
10.   Dallin H. Oaks and Warren Lehman, *A Criminal Justice System and the Indigent* (Chicago: University of Chicago Press, 1968), p. 80. See interpretation of this material in Stephen L. Wasby, *The Impact of the United States Supreme Court* (Homewood, Illinois: Dorsey Press, 1970), chapter 5.
11.   Jacob, *Justice in America*, pp. 168–69.
12.   Charles Ares, Anne Rankin, and Herbert Sturz, "The Manhattan Bail Project: An Interim Report on the Use of Pre-trial Parole," *New York University Law Review* 38 (1963), pp. 82-84.
13.   President's Commission on Law Enforcement and the Administration of Justice, *Task Force Report: The Administration of Justice* (Washington, D.C.: GPO, 1967). Discussed in Kaplan, pp. 320–35.
14.   Kaplan, p. 323.
15.   Urban Research Corporation, *Preventive Detention* (Chicago: Urban Research Corporation, 1971), p. 60. Also discussed in Kaplan, pp. 324–27.
16.   Richard A. Watson, *Office of Attorney General* (Columbia: Missouri Studies No. 1, University of Missouri, 1962), pp. 19–22.

17. Herbert Jacob, "Politics and Criminal Prosecution in New Orleans," in Kenneth N. Vines and Herbert Jacob, *Studies in Judicial Politics* (New Orleans, Tulane Studies in Political Science, vol. 8 1963), pp. 77–98. See discussion in Jacob, *Justice in America*, pp. 171–76.

18. Wasby, p. 148.

19. Kaplan, p. 572.

20. 384 U.S. 436 (1966).

21. Michael S. Wald, et al., "Interrogations in New Haven: The Impact of Miranda," in *The Impact of Supreme Court Decisions,* edited by Theodore Becker (New York: Oxford University Press, 1969), p. 154.

22. Ibid.

23. Ibid., pp. 156–57.

24. Richard J. Medalie, Leonard Zeitz, and Paul Alexander, "Custodial Police Interrogation in Our Nation's Capital: The Attempt to Implement *Miranda,*" in Becker, p. 174.

25. Ibid., pp. 170–71.

26. *Mapp v. Ohio,* 367 U.S. 643 (1961).

27. Stuart S. Nagel, *The Legal Process from a Behavioral Perspective* (Homewood, Illinois: Dorsey Press, 1969), pp. 308–12.

28. Wasby, p. 148; quotes James Q. Wilson, *Varieties of Police Behavior* (Cambridge, Mass.: Harvard University Press, 1968), pp. 286, 293.

29. Kaplan, pp. 77–78.

30. Cole, pp. 315–35.

31. Kaplan, pp. 77–78.

7. CIVIL JUSTICE POLICY

1. Charles G. Howard and Robert S. Summers, *Law: Its Nature, Functions, and Limits* (Englewood Cliffs, N.J.: Prentice-Hall, Inc., 1965), parts 2 and 3, pp. 303–337.

2. Martin Shapiro, "From Public Law to Public Policy, or The 'Public' in 'Public Law,'" *PS* 5 (1972): 410.

3. Ibid., p. 411.

4. Ibid., p. 410.

5. Harold J. Grilliot, *Introduction to Law and the Legal System* (Boston: Houghton Mifflin Co., 1975), pp. 197–99.

6. Herbert Jacob, *Justice in America* (Boston: Little, Brown and Co., 1972), p. 181–82.

7. Marvin R. Summer, "Analysis of Factors that Influence Choice of Forum in Diversity Cases," *Iowa Law Review* 47 (1962): 937.

8. Grilliot, p. 209.

9. Ibid., pp. 211–12.

10. Jacob, pp. 184–85.

11. Ibid. See also Maurice Rosenbery, *The Pre-Trial Conference and Effective Justice* (New York: Columbia University Press, 1964).

12. James Eisenstein, *Politics and the Legal Process* (New York: Harper & Row, 1973), pp. 270–75.

13. Jerome Carlin, Jan Howard, and Sheldon Messinger, *Civil Justice and the Poor* (New York: Russell Sage Foundation, 1967), pp. 30, 37, 131.

14. Eisenstein, p. 263.

15. Ibid., pp. 269–70.

16. Jacob, p. 187.

8. ADJUDICATION OF POLICY ISSUES

1. David Truman, *The Governmental Process: Political Interests and Public Opinion* (New York: Alfred A. Knopf, 1951), pp. x–xi.
2. Jerome Hall, "Unification of Political and Legal Theory," *Political Science Quarterly* 69 (1954): 15–28.
3. Jack W. Peltason, *Federal Courts in the Political Process* (Garden City, New York: Doubleday, 1955), p. 3.
4. Victor G. Rosenblum, *Law as a Political Instrument* (New York: Random House, 1955), pp. 1–4.
5. Herbert Jacob, *Justice in America* (Boston: Little, Brown and Co., 1972), p. 35.
6. Samuel Krislov, "The Amicus Curiae Brief: From Friendship to Advocacy," *Yale Law Journal* 72 (1963): 716.
7. Jacob, p. 36.
8. 416 U.S. 312 (1974).
9. For a current and informed analysis of the political implications of standing see Karen Orren, "Standing to Sue: Interest Group Conflict in the Federal Courts," *American Political Science Review* 70 (1976): 723–41.
10. Fed. R. Civ. P. 23 (a) and (b).
11. 94 S. Ct. 2140 (1974).
12. Kenneth W. Dam, "Class Action Notice: Who Needs It?" *1974 Supreme Court Review* (1975), p. 98.
13. Stuart S. Nagel, *The Legal Process from a Behavioral Perspective* (Homewood, Illinois: Dorsey Press, 1969), p. vii.
14. *Brown v. Board of Education,* 347 U.S. 483 (1954).
15. *Baker v. Carr,* 369 U.S. 186 (1962).
16. *Douglas v. California,* 372 U.S. 355 (1963).
17. Edwin W. Tucker, *Adjudication of Social Issues* (St. Paul, Minnesota: West Publishing Co., 1971), pp. 38–39.
18. Ibid., p. 40.
19. Ibid.
20. 423 F. 2d 469 (1970).
21. Werner F. Grumbaum, *Judicial Policymaking: The Supreme Court and Environmental Quality* (Morristown, N.J.: General Learning Press, 1976), p. 11.
22. Ibid., pp. 29–31.
23. Tucker, p. 157.
24. Ibid., pp. 158–60.
25. Jerry Alan Green and Ellen Sickles Green, "The Legal Profession and the Process of Social Change," *Hastings Law Journal* 21 (1970): 589.
26. Ibid., p. 575.
27. C. Thomas Dienes, "To Feed the Hungry: Judicial Retrenchment in Welfare Adjudication," *California Law Review* 58 (1970): 555.
28. 397 U.S. 471 (1970).
29. Dienes, 555–59.
30. Frederick M. Wirt, *Politics of Southern Equality: Law and Social Change in a Mississippi County* (Chicago: Aldine, 1970), pp. 4–5.
31. Ibid., p. 8.
32. Gordon W. Allport, "You Can Legislate Morality," in Frederick M. Wirt and Willis D. Hawley, eds., *New Dimensions of Freedom in America* (San Francisco: Chandler, 1969), p. 263.
33. Ibid., p. 264.
34. Ibid., p. 263.
35. 383 U.S. 463 (1966).
36. James P. Levine, "Constitutional Law and Obscene Literature: An Investigation of Bookseller Censorship Practices," in Theodore Becker, ed., *The Impact*

of Supreme Court Decisions (New York: Oxford University Press, 1969), p. 140.

37.   John H. Kessel, "Public Perceptions of the Supreme Court," *Midwest Journal of Political Science* 10 (1966): 171.

38.   William K. Muir, Jr., *Prayer in the Public Schools: Law and Attitude Change* (Chicago: University of Chicago Press, 1967).

39.   347 U.S. 483 (1954).

40.   Alexander Bickel, *The Least Dangerous Branch* (Indianapolis: Bobbs-Merrill Co., 1962), p. 246.

41.   Peltason, p. 10.

42.   Jacob, pp. 5-9.

43.   Quoted from Chief Justice Burger's speech dedicating the Georgetown Univeristy Law Center, *The Washington Post* (Saturday, September 18, 1971), p. B1.

44.   Gerald Garvey, *Constitutional Bricolage* (Princeton, N.J.: Princeton University Press, 1971).

9. JURISPRUDENCE AND JURISCIENCE

1.   See his work which has been republished as Marquis de Laplace, *A Philosophical Essay on Probabilities* (New York: Dover Publications, 1952).

2.   Yehezdel Dror, *Ventures in Policy Sciences: Concepts and Applications* (New York: American Elsevier Publishing Co., 1971), pp. 167-203.

3.   Stuart S. Nagel, *The Legal Process from a Behavioral Perspective* (Homewood, Ill.: Dorsey Press, 1969), pp. 39-41.

4.   Yehezdel Dror, *Public Policymaking Reexamined* (Scranton, Pa.: Chandler, 1968), pp. 240-45.

5.   Dror, *Ventures in Policy Sciences,* pp. 167, 169-70.

6.   Ibid., p. 181.

7.   Lawrence M. Friedman and Stewart Macaulay, eds., *Law and the Behavioral Sciences* (Indianapolis: Bobbs-Merrill, 1969), p. 1.

8.   Irving Louis Horowitz and James Everett Katz, *Social Science and Public Policy in the United States* (New York: Praeger Publishers, 1975), p. 45.

INDEX

ABOUT THE AUTHOR

Dr. William C. Louthan is an Associate Professor of Politics and Government and Co-Director of the Midwest Institute of Social Research at Ohio Wesleyan University. He has written numerous articles on judicial politics, criminal justice policy, and elections policy published in a variety of professional journals.